BEAUTIFUL BRUSHSTROKES
STEP BY STEP

Maureen McNaughton, CDA

NORTH LIGHT BOOKS
CINCINNATI, OHIO
www.artistsnetwork.com

Other fine North Light Books are available from your local bookstore, art supply store or direct from the publisher.

07 06 05 04 03   5 4 3 2 1

Library of Congress Cataloging-in-Publication Data

McNaughton, Maureen
  Beautiful brushstrokes : step by step / Maureen McNaughton
    p. cm.
  Includes index.
  ISBN 1-58180-381-8 (pbk. : alk. paper)
  1. Painting--Technique. 2. Brushwork. 3. Folk art.
  4. Decoration and ornament. I. Title.

TT385.M38 2003
745.7'23--dc21   2003042140

Editors: Christine Doyle and Holly Davis
Production Coordinator: Kristen Heller
Designer: Joanna Detz
Layout Artist: John Langan
Photographer: Christine Polomsky

metric conversion chart

TO CONVERT	TO	MULTIPLY BY
Inches	Centimeters	2.54
Centimeters	Inches	0.4
Feet	Centimeters	30.5
Centimeters	Feet	0.03
Yards	Meters	0.9
Meters	Yards	1.1
Sq. Inches	Sq. Centimeters	6.45
Sq. Centimeters	Sq. Inches	0.16
Sq. Feet	Sq. Meters	0.09
Sq. Meters	Sq. Feet	10.8
Sq. Yards	Sq. Meters	0.8
Sq. Meters	Sq. Yards	1.2
Pounds	Kilograms	0.45
Kilograms	Pounds	2.2
Ounces	Grams	28.4
Grams	Ounces	0.04

About the Author

Maureen McNaughton, CDA with Master Stroke certification, began her teaching career in Canada in 1974 and was teaching internationally by 1980. She is known for her ability to make complex techniques easy and understandable, with her instruction appearing in books, pattern packets, videos and countless magazine articles.

Maureen teaches several seminars per season in her Belwood, Ontario, studio as well as a few seminars a year on the road. She is also a sought-after lecturer on teaching methods. As an appointee to the Society of Decorative Painters Task Force on Excellence in Teaching, she helped develop the Teacher Development Program, launched in 2001 to raise teaching standards through training and evaluation.

Maureen is a working artist as well as a teacher and trainer. In 1996 she was the convention artist for the British Association of Decorative and Folk Arts Tudor Rose convention in London. In 2000, Maureen's work began regularly enhancing columns and departments of *The Decorative Painter* magazine.

In addition to her teaching, training and painting, she has improved the "tools of the trade" with her Maureen McNaughton line of brushes, designed "by an artist for an artist."

Maureen is an active and supportive member of three international associations: the Canadian Decorative Artists Network, the British Association of Decorative and Folk Arts and the National Society of Tole and Decorative Painters.

Acknowledgments

Developing a book requires the hard work of so many people. A big thank you to my tireless editors, Christine Doyle and Holly Davis at North Light, who directed and pulled this whole book together.

Thanks also to Kathy Kipp, who first came to me with the idea for this book. Her enthusiasm for this project and guidance in developing the outline made the job so much easier.

Stan Clifford from DecoArt has never failed with his generosity and support through the years. Thank you, Stan.

Merci beaucoup to Jacques Bérubé and Manon Larose of La Maison BeL'art for supplying their expertly handmade bentwood pieces, which I love to paint on.

Pam Hawkins and Chris Wallace from Walnut Hollow were most generous in providing a wide variety of surfaces to choose from for the projects in the book. Thank you both.

Thank you to Jo Lutness from Painters Paradise, who scours the globe for unusual surfaces, which always inspire me.

If you enjoy decorative painting, you may wish to become a member in the following organizations:

The Society of Decorative Painters
393 N. McLean Blvd.
Wichita, KS 67203-5968
USA
www.decorativepainters.org

The Canadian Decorative Artists Network
4981 Hwy. #7 East, Unit 12A Suite 253
Markham, ON L3R 1N1
Canada
www.cdan.com

The British Association of Decorative & Folk Arts
Margaret Nelson, BADFA Membership Secretary
6 Falcon Road
Horndean Waterloo
Hants England PO8 9BY
United Kingdom

Dedication

This book is dedicated to my husband, Jim, and our children, Graeme and Laura— my partners in this life journey. Your love means more to me than mere words can say.

Table of Contents

Introduction

I will never forget the first time I saw an artist pull a brushstroke. I was mesmerized. Imagine my excitement at seeing a two-toned shape created with just one stroke of the brush. Then I watched those brushstrokes combine to create a beautiful flower before my eyes. It was magic! I knew right there and then what I wanted to do with my life. By teaching brushstrokes to others, I could relive that excitement again and again through the eyes of my students.

Brushstrokes create specific shapes with one stroke of the brush, using pressure and release to form the shapes. By double loading the brush, one can create highlight or shading simultaneously within the stroke. These shapes are then combined, much like pieces in a puzzle, to create beautiful designs.

Through the ages, strokework has been a popular form of folk art in many countries, especially in Europe. In North America, we benefit from our ancestors and have adapted many aspects of their painting to ours.

I found that my own self-study eventually led me toward creating unconventional brushstrokes. With these shapes I was able to develop more realistic and fluid floral paintings, compared to what I had achieved in the past with traditional brushstrokes. The round brush became my brush of choice because it affords me greater freedom to create these unusual strokes.

My next challenge was to devise a loading technique that could accomplish more than just creating a shape with the brushstroke. My goal was to create the growth direction lines I had observed in every petal and leaf and to also lay down a value change within the stroke. During this experimental phase, I noticed that whenever there were ridges on the sides of the brushstroke, the buildup was consistently the loading color. This was the clue that the loading method had to allow the painter to control the amount and distribution of loading color within the brush. With these objectives in mind, I developed my tipping technique, which has proved to be easily mastered with a little practice.

Even after all these years, I have yet to do a painting in which every stroke is perfect. For the most part, I will repair a poor stroke instead of wiping it off. Making errors is inevitable. Your artistic skills will grow every time you identify what is wrong and then take the steps needed to develop a solution. In this book I share with you some of the techniques I use to fix my strokes.

I encourage you to invest a little time learning the loading technique and all the different strokes. Then begin with the roses-and-tulips projects (heart basket and floral corner shelf). With the variety of design and color options provided, this study will be fun and productive, and it is the springboard to the remaining projects. Have fun!

CHAPTER ONE

Materials

Brushes

In 1978 I introduced my line of McNaughton brushes. They have evolved through the years as my understanding of brush capabilities has grown. The unique construction of the synthetic filament used in my brushes is designed to carry the large amount of paint required for my technique with even distribution through the brush. Their spring and resilience make these brushes ideal for strokework.

Round The round brushes are full-bodied but come to a very sharp point. They are used for plump strokes. The sizes used in this book are no. 2, no. 4, no. 6 and no. 8.

Toler The toler has the body of the round brush, but the length and tapering of a liner. It is used for long slender strokes. The sizes used in this book are no. 5 and no. 9.

Liner The liner is a longer brush that tapers to a very sharp point. It is used for line work, detail and some brushstrokes. The sizes used in this book are no. 00 and no. 02.

Philbert This is a flat brush that comes to a point, as opposed to filberts, which have a domed top. The philbert's shape allows you to start the stroke with a point and to finish it with a thin, curved tail. Philberts are also ideal for short, wide brushstrokes. The sizes used in this book are no. 4 and no. 6.

Flat In my brush line I have three lengths of flat ferruled brushes that all close to a tight, firm chisel edge. The longer length shader is used for large strokes and for shading long lengths. Blenders are quite short and may be used for floating color in tight areas or for blending a stiffer-bodied paint such as oils or alkyds. Flats are the middle length and are the ones I use for floated color in the projects in this book. The sizes I call for are no. 6, no. 10, and no. 12.

Maureen McNaughton Brushes (top to bottom): round, toler, liner, philbert, flat, Professional 200 Series round, Genesis scrubbie, mop, basecoat/varnish flat.

The 2-inch (51mm) flat was originally designed for teachers to demonstrate in a large format in class. However, I also use this brush for faux finishes, basecoating and varnishing.

McNaughton Professional 200 Series These brushes are made from a flexible natural hair. Available in both flats and rounds, these brushes have a dense construction to create their full-bodied shape. In this book, the rounds are used for stippling when a softer effect is desired. Many artists also use the Professionals for dry brushing, oil rouging and canvas painting.

McNaughton Genesis Scrubbie Some of you may own a scrubbie brush from my Genesis series, which may be used for stippling. This Genesis line has been replaced with the 200 Series McNaughton Professional Brushes. In this book, when you see a McNaughton Professional brush used for stippling, you may substitute a McNaughton Genesis Scrubbie of similar size; however, the scrubbie will produce a less soft stipple.

Mop The mop, made from very soft natural hair, is a full, flat brush with a domed top. Use a mop to soften the faint edge of floated color or to stretch the color out with a gentle sweep. Sizes no. 0 and no. 1 are used in this book.

Basecoat/Varnish Flat This 1-inch (25mm) flat brush is most commonly used for applying acrylic basecoat and varnish.

Paint and Mediums

DecoArt Americana Acrylics These acrylics are non-toxic water-based and come in a wide variety of colors. Use them as they come from the bottle for basecoating. For strokework, add a drop or two of my extender to most colors for effortless and beautifully blended brushstrokes.

Extender This is the key ingredient that makes the DecoArt paint blend into soft directional lines in my tipping technique. It also allows you to stretch the stroke as long as needed and still create sharp points when required.

The recipe for this extender is the result of many hours of experimenting with numerous acrylic mediums. To make extender, combine three parts water with one part DecoArt Easy Float in a clean 2-ounce (56.8g) bottle.

Add one or two drops of extender to a 1-inch (25mm) puddle of paint. As you mix it into the paint, you will feel the viscosity loosen. Some colors do not require extender, and this is indicated with an asterisk (*) in the list of colors for each project. Visit my Web site (see Resources on page 126) for a list of all the DecoArt colors that require extender for strokework and the ones that do not.

Varnish For the projects in this book I used DecoArt DuraClear Satin or Gloss Varnish. These are brush-on water-based polyurethane varnishes that produce a tough, flexible, nonyellowing, weatherproof finish.

Other Materials

Wet palette The success of my technique depends on keeping the acrylic paint at the correct consistency and open on the palette for as long as possible. A wet palette can be made with any shallow container. When I travel, I set up my wet palette on a large sheet of Plexiglas because it takes up little room in the suitcase.

McNaughton Wet Palette Paper prevents the water from seeping into the acrylic yet keeps the viscosity of the paint consistent for many hours. See pages 18-19 for instructions on my method for setting up a wet palette.

Disposable wax palette This is a book of tear-off coated paper sheets. Pour basecoat colors, faux finish colors and varnish on this palette. When a project calls for color mixing, do it on this palette and then transfer to the wet palette. Make sure the palette you chose appears to have a shiny coating so it will not absorb the moisture from the acrylic.

Krylon leafing pens These valuable tools have flat-shaped, hard felt nibs. I used the gold and silver pens in this book. Particles of metal are suspended in a lacquer base, which produces a highly reflective metallic finish. When dragged along an edge, the pen produces a perfect line that echoes the shape of the edge.

Always shake the pen before using. Then plunge the nib up and down on a hard surface to activate the pen. Allow the applied metal leafing to dry thoroughly. Then protect with brush-on varnish. Do not use a spray over unprotected metal leafing. The lacquer in the spray would activate the lacquer in the leafing, causing the metallic particles to settle and no longer reflect the light.

Gold leaf This is a very thin sheet of imitation gold that is applied to the surface with a special leafing adhesive. The adhesive is applied with an old brush. See pages 65-66 for step-by-step pictures and instructions on applying this product.

Cotton swabs These swabs are used for pouncing color in the fluffy fillers found in many of the projects in this book. Look for swabs that are nicely rounded and not too fuzzy. For smaller areas, use the pointed cosmetic swab. Dip the end of the dry swab in color and pounce out the excess on the palette.

Brush basin I prefer the rectangular Loew-Cornell brush basin because it has a large area for brush cleaning. There are ridges on the floor on one side of the tub. To clean the brush, drag the ferrule across the ridges in one direction to vibrate out any stubborn color.

I urge you not to leave your brushes in the basin for any length of time. Synthetic hair does not have a memory. Brushes left in the water blossom open, and often the tips are bent. This soon becomes the new shape of the brush, which makes it useless for strokework. Brushes in tiptop condition are the most important tools you own, so take the time to clean them, and return them to their intended shape after each washing.

Palette knife I prefer a metal bent-blade knife because it scrapes up every last drop of color. Loew-Cornell makes a number of excellent knives in this style.

Soft absorbent paper towel You will quickly ruin your brushes if you wipe them across a coarse rough towel. I prefer blue shop cloth, found where automotive supplies are sold, or white Scott Rags, found with house painting supplies.

Wet wipes Pour $1/4$ cup of rubbing alcohol into a new container of wipes for fast hand cleanup. Alcohol will dissolve even dried acrylic paint.

White and gray chalk pencils Occasionally a pattern line may be lost, or you may want to add to the design. I use chalk pencils for this because the marks remove easily with an eraser or a damp cloth. Sharpened school chalk can also be used.

Stylus tool This tool is used for painting dots.

Light and dark transfer paper This paper has a dark or light coating. Place it coated side down on the surface under the pattern to transfer the pattern. For a faint pattern line, remove excess coating from the paper with a dry paper towel.

Tracing paper Use this transparent paper when copying patterns.

Plastic wrap Inexpensive plastic wrap is used in many of the faux finishes in this book.

Brush cleaner At the end of the painting day, I use Deco-Magic Brush Cleaner or rubbing alcohol to dissolve any stubborn acrylic still left in the brush.

Wood filler Use this water-based product to fill holes and dents in a wood surface before sealing.

Sanding ovals These ovals are very convenient and come in a variety of grits for removing rough edges and smoothing surface imperfections.

Tack cloth This is a sticky cloth used to remove wood dust or paint erasures from the surface after sanding.

Bondo spreader This flexible plastic spatula-type tool is available where automotive supplies are sold. I use it when preparing my wet palette to express excess water. It is also used to burnish edges of tape when doing stripes.

Frosted "invisible" tape There are many brands on the market, but choose one that removes easily. This tape is used for masking off stripes. Burnish the edges of the tape with a Bondo spreader or eraser.

Eraser I prefer the Koh-I-Noor gum eraser to remove visible graphite lines when the painting is completed.

Pencil Mechanical pencils are always sharp.

Scissors

Ruler

CHAPTER TWO

Preparation & Painting Techniques

Surface Preparation

1] Use wood filler to fill surface dents, nail holes or places where two wood pieces don't meet. Most wood fillers are water-based and dry quickly. Scoop a small amount from the jar with the palette knife and replace the lid. Hold the palette knife on an angle to spread the filler over the hole or imperfection. Clean the knife as soon as you are done using it.

2] Let this dry several hours or overnight. Sand the filler level to the surface with a sanding oval or fine sandpaper. Remove all dust with a tack cloth.

3] Seal the MDF (medium-density fiberboard) or wood surface before sanding the edges. Seal tin, MDF or close-grained wood with Multi-Purpose Sealer. Seal wood with a wide-open grain with gesso. Allow this to dry naturally or force dry with a hair dryer.

4] The sealer will raise the wood grain, so sand the surface smooth. Remove all dust with a tack cloth.

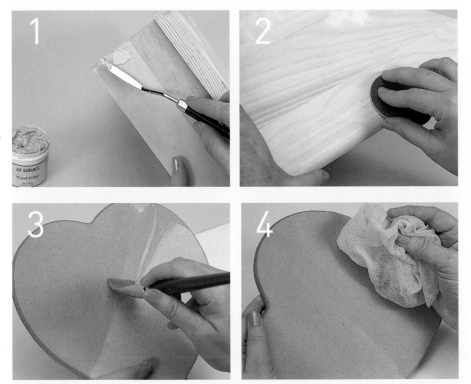

Surface Preparation, continued

5] One option is to apply the acrylic with the basecoat/varnish brush. Load the brush on the palette. Work on a small area at a time and brush the color with firm short strokes to push the color into the surface. Smooth any brush marks in this area with lighter pressure before moving on. Repeat as required for opaque coverage.

6] The acrylic may also raise the wood grain. When the surface is completely dry, sand it again. Remove all dust with a tack cloth.

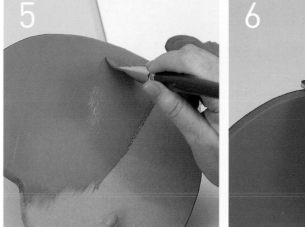

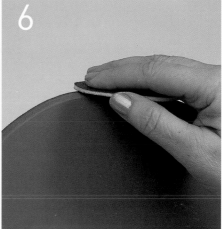

Basecoating: Another Method

Another option is to basecoat with a sponge roller. Use the roller dry. With firm pressure, roll color out from the edge of the paint puddle on the palette.

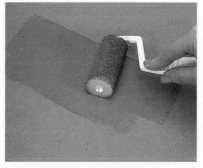

With firm pressure, roll the color on the surface. Bubbles will form as you push the paint into the pores of the surface.

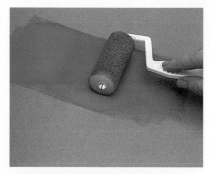

Keep rolling over the surface but with a lighter pressure to smooth out the bubbles. Allow to dry. Then repeat as required for opaque coverage.

Transferring the Pattern

1. Photocopy the pattern or trace it onto tracing paper. To secure the pattern to the surface, I first cut a small hole in the pattern. Position the pattern on the surface and place a piece of tape over the hole.

2. Slip transfer paper between the pattern and the surface. Then place another piece of tracing paper over the pattern and tape it to the pattern. Trace along all pattern lines with a pencil. This allows me to see exactly what has been transferred.

3. In strokework, the pattern is just a guideline. So when I transfer patterns, I don't trace over every line. For example, in this tulip leaf I transferred only an arrow up the middle of the leaf. Also, I did not trace on the turned edges of the rose leaf. Without the confines of the pattern, my leaf and turned edge will take the shape of the brushstroke.

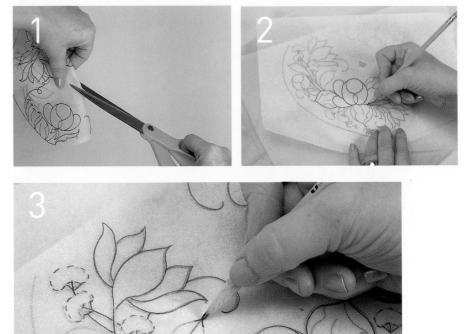

Floating Techniques

Loading the Brush for Floating

1 First wet the flat brush in water and blot well on a paper towel. Then touch just the tip of the chisel edge into extender.

2 Work this amount of extender along the length of the bristles with firm pressure. Turn the brush over and repeat. If the brush feels dry at this stage, pick up more extender. If it feels too "juicy," blot the tip on a paper towel.

3 Dip the corner edge of the brush into the paint.

4 Place the brush firmly on the surface. With the handle slanted back toward you, push forward on the bristles.

5 Maintain pressure as you pull down.

6 Turn the brush over and repeat on the other side.

Narrow Float

[1] To produce a narrow float, dip only a small portion of the corner into the paint puddle.

[2] Blend on the palette as described and paint the narrow float on the surface.

Wide Float

[1] For a wider float, dip a larger portion of the corner edge into the paint puddle.

[2] Blend on the palette and apply the wide float on the surface. You can walk the color out for an even wider float.

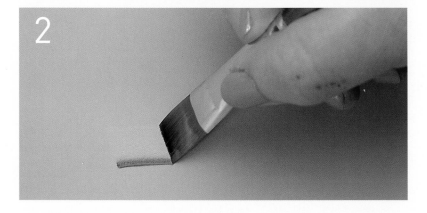

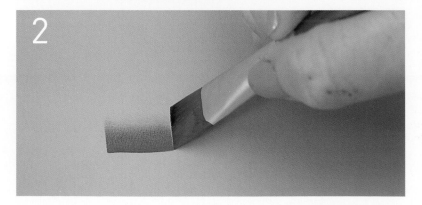

Floated C-Stroke on a Dry Surface

[1] Floating on a dry surface produces strong color. Set the chisel down and slide to the left with no pressure. Pull down toward you in a curved path. Apply slight pressure here to soften the float.

[2] Relax back up onto the chisel and slide over to the right to complete the C.

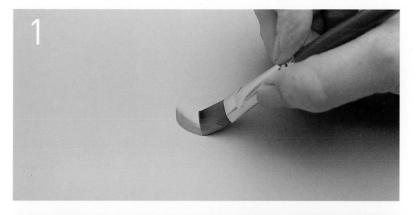

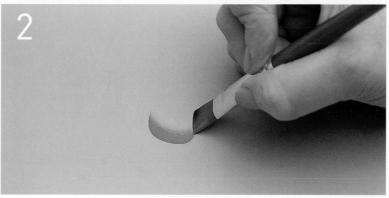

Floated C-Stroke on a Damp Surface

[1] Floating on a surface dampened with extender lengthens the open time of the paint so you can manipulate the color for a streaked or soft effect. Paint the C-stroke as explained above.

[2] While still wet, use the chisel edge to coax out many fine streaks.

[3] Here is the finished effect. Note the fine lines along the entire faint edge of the float.

[4] Another option is to soften the faint edge of the float by lightly mopping the color outward with a dry mop brush.

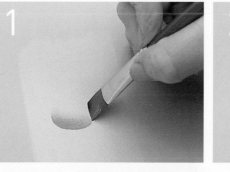

Angular Float on a Leaf

To create leaf veins, paint angular-shaped floats that allow the spaces between the floats to act as veins.

1 | Set the chisel on a 45° angle to the center vein. Slide over toward the center vein, but not quite to it. Pull the floated stroke beside the center vein for a short distance. You can walk the color out for a deeper float.

2 | Slide the chisel on a 45° angle away from the center vein to complete this stroke. Soften the faint edges with the mop if required.

3 | Continue to paint angular floats, leaving open spaces to represent the veins.

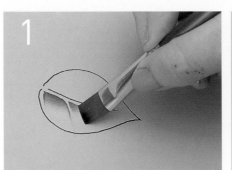
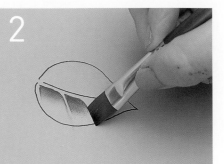
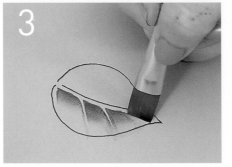

V-Shaped Float

Shadows are the darkest in V-shaped areas. This example shows a shadow placed on a leaf, between overlapping flower petals.

1 | Begin the float with the color corner of the flat brush in the V. Stroke across the area, walking the color out into the leaf.

2 | With a gentle pat-and-pull motion, apply the float across the area and continue to walk the color out as far as desired.

3 | Soften the faint edge of the float by lightly mopping the color outward with a dry mop brush.

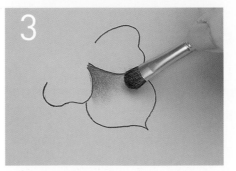
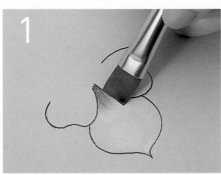
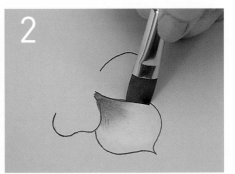

Float to Create a Turned Edge

1. Draw the shape of the turned edge onto the petal with a chalk pencil.

2. Float the shading color under the turned edge. Walk the color out.

3. Line the edge of the turn with the tipping color used in the brushstroke. Extend the line past the shaded area, along the sides of the stroke.

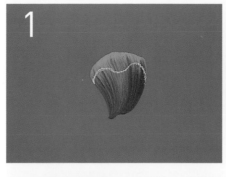

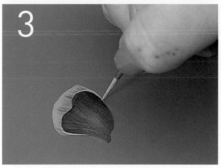

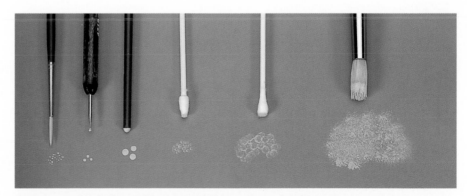

Stippling

Stippling refers to the action of pouncing up and down. Different tools offer a variety of effects.

Brush Load the entire brush. Gently touch the tip to the surface. A liner brush will produce irregular-shaped dots. Stippling with the chisel of a flat brush will produce a line.

Stylus This tool may be double-ended with a small metal ball at one end and a larger ball at the other end. Dip the tool into the paint. Touch the surface to produce a perfectly round dot. Continue to touch the surface without reloading to produce dots that get progressively smaller.

Brush handle Use a brush handle as you would a stylus tool to produce larger dots.

Different tools produce different stippled effects. From left to right: liner brush, stylus, brush handle, pointed cotton swab, regular cotton swab, China bristle brush.

Cotton Swabs Look for swabs that are tightly wound and not too fuzzy. Dip the end into color. Pounce out the excess on the palette until you see a soft ring of color.

Pointed cotton swabs are found in drug store cosmetic departments. They produce a smaller ring. Regular cotton swabs make a larger ring.

China bristle brush This stiff bristle produces a soft speckled effect or a heavy one, depending on how much color is carried in the brush. Dip the brush tip into color. Pounce out the excess on a dry paper towel.

McNaughton Professional 200 Series rounds create a stipple similar to the China bristle, but softer.

CHAPTER THREE

Basic Brushstrokes

Successful brushstrokes depend on so many things happening before you even set the brush on your surface.

One is to keep the "fresh from the bottle" consistency of the acrylics. These paints are formulated to dry quickly, but storing them on a wet palette will slow the process considerably. In this chapter you are shown the step-by-step process of setting up this palette.

Loading the brush properly is the key to beautiful blending in the brushstroke and to the success of the stroke itself. Don't rush through this step. This chapter leads you through the method of loading the brush in a controlled fashion that guarantees even distribution of paint within the entire brush.

You will learn that the shape of a brushstroke is created with the application and release of pressure. You can curve the stroke, pull it straight or fan the brush open. Practice the strokes on paper before going to the surface. It will give you the confidence to paint the projects with enthusiasm and joy.

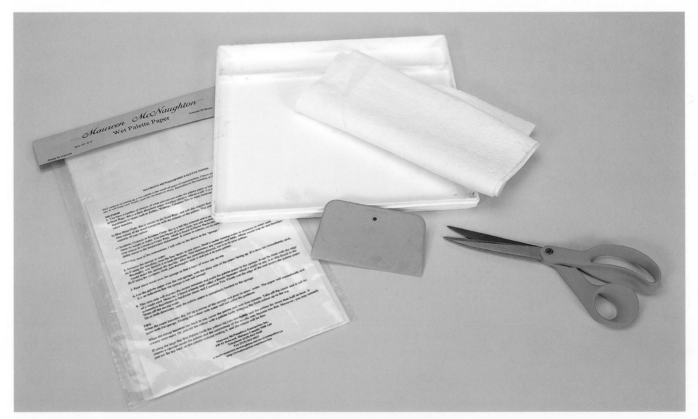

Materials required for my wet palette setup are McNaughton Wet Palette Paper, palette container, white Scott Rags toweling (or blue shop cloth), Bondo Spreader (or old credit card) and scissors.

Setting up a Wet Palette

1] Place four layers of toweling in water, keeping them together as one unit. Without wringing, stretch the toweling in both directions to remove any wrinkles.

2] Place the stretched toweling in the palette and cut to fit.

3] Pour more water over the toweling.

4] Place a sheet of palette paper on the wet toweling. Wait for the water to soak in and wrinkle the paper.

5] With firm pressure, pull the edge of the Bondo tool or credit card across the palette paper to smooth it to the toweling and remove excess water.

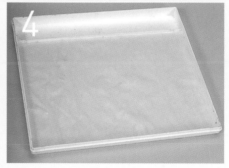

Loading the Brush

1. Make the extender in an empty plastic squeeze bottle. Divide the bottle lengthwise in fourths. Fill one fourth with Easy Float. Fill the rest of the bottle with water.

2. Put out the paint in 1-inch (25mm) puddles, with 1 inch to 2 inches (25mm to 51mm) of open space between the puddles. Add one drop of extender to those colors indicated to make the paints the same consistency. Mix the extender into the paint with a palette knife.

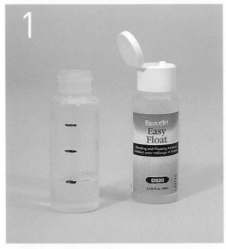

3. Dampen the brush with water. Press the brush down to the ferrule on a soft paper towel to remove excess water.

4. Pull a small amount of paint from the edge of the puddle into the loading zone. With firm pressure, work the paint into the brush, right down to the ferrule. There must be paint on the entire length of the bristles in order for the brush to open in the stroke.

5. Turn the brush over and repeat on the opposite side. If the brush drags or feels too dry, pull more color into the loading zone.

6. With no pressure, stroke all sides of the brush in the loading zone to shape it into its round shape. Do not roll or twist the brush.

Loading the Brush, continued

[7] Remove paint from all around the tip of the brush by dragging it across a sharp edge, such as the edge of the palette. This makes bare bristles on which the tipping color will grab.

[8] Stir the tip of the brush in the tipping color. Dip in shallowly for a short stroke and more deeply for a long stroke.

[9] Gently touch the tip of the brush on the palette to break the surface tension between the two colors on the brush and remove excess tipping color.

[10] After painting the stroke, wipe any residual tipping color from the brush on a soft paper towel. Then reload in the loading color. This prevents contaminating the loading color. Remember to repeat this entire loading process for every brushstroke.

Troubleshooting

Here I have too much paint in the loading zone. Use the palette knife to push all color back into the puddle. Then start again.

Painting the Strokes

Hand Position

Hold the brush with your fingers positioned on the ferrule as they would be on a pencil. Have your baby finger down for support, but raise your wrist off the surface. Your forearm may rest on the table. Direct the handle toward the ceiling.

Brush Handle Position

1 The approach phase is right before you touch the surface. Note that the handle is pointed back toward you.

2 When pressure is applied, position the handle perpendicular to the surface.

3 As you sweep the brush off the surface, arc the handle away from you.

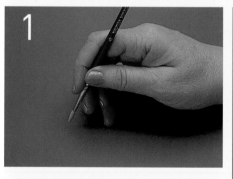

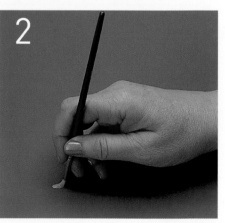

Pressure Strokes

Pressure strokes are wonderful for filling in round shapes while producing beautiful streaking.

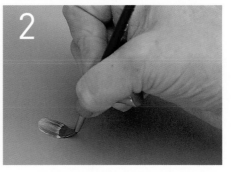

Straight Pressure Stroke

1 Lay the brush firmly on the surface. Pause to allow the brush to open.

2 Pull the brush straight toward you.

3 Slightly taper the end of the stroke by releasing pressure on the brush.

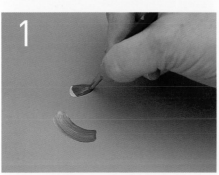

Curved Pressure Stroke

1 Lay the brush firmly on the surface. Pause.

2 Pull the brush along a curved path, in this case to the right.

3 Slightly taper the end of the stroke by releasing pressure.

Pressure Stroke
Flat on One Side

1 Lay the brush firmly on the surface. Pause.

2 Fan the bristles out to the left and begin to pull. Keep the right side of the stroke flat.

3 Slightly taper the end of the stroke.

4 Reload. Press and fan the brush out to the right. Keep the left side of the stroke flat.

5 Slightly taper the end of the stroke by releasing pressure.

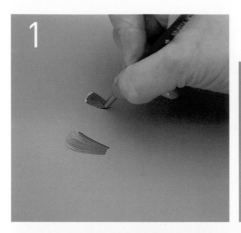

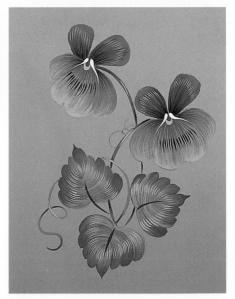

The yellow petals on these Johnny-jump-ups are made with pressure strokes that are flat on one side. The leaves are made with curved pressure strokes (page 23). See pages 72-91 for the complete project.

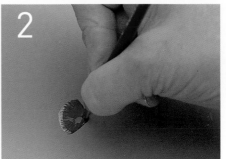

Fanned Pressure Stroke

¹] Pull the point.

²] Apply pressure, fanning out the bristles on one side only.

³] Pull the brush and slightly taper the end.

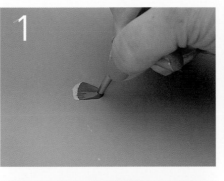

Fanned Pressure Stroke with Philbert

For short strokes use a brush with short bristles. Use the philbert the same way as the round.

¹] Lay the brush down to the fer-rule and fan open.

²] Pull the brush and slightly taper the end of the stroke by releasing pressure.

Fanned pressure strokes made with a no. 6 round brush were used to create the rear petals of these calla lilies. See pages 104-121 for the complete project.

Tapered Pressure Stroke

1 Begin like a straight pressure stroke (page 23). Start releasing pressure gradually as the brush begins to move toward you.

2 Continue to pull and lift the brush to taper the stroke and finish with a blunt end.

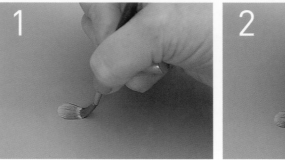

Bumpy Pressure Stroke

1 Pull out the top of the stroke with little pressure.

2 Lay the brush down with the ferrule on the surface. Fan it open.

3 Begin to pull the stroke and taper the end by releasing pressure on the brush.

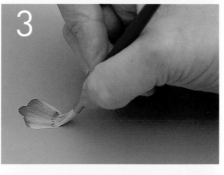

Some of the rear petals of this rhododendron are made with bumpy pressure strokes. See page 124 for the complete design.

Pointed Pressure Strokes

Pointed pressure strokes begin with a point. For variation, you can try curving the stroke or fanning it out on one side.

Pointed Pressure Stroke

1] Pull a point with the tip of the brush.

2] Press the brush down.

3] Pull and taper the end of the stroke.

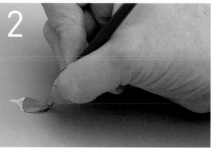

Curved Pointed Pressure Stroke

1] Pull the point, press and begin to pull the stroke on a curved path, in this case to the right.

2] Continue the curved path and slightly taper the end.

S-Shaped Variation

Pull the point, press and pull the stroke on a curved path in one direction, in this case to the right. Then change direction to form an S-shaped path.

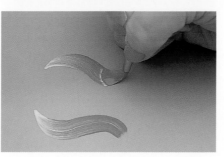

Pointed Pressure Stroke
Flat on One Side

1] Pull the point.

2] Apply pressure, fanning out the bristles on one side only.

3] Pull the brush and slightly taper the end.

4] To form a petal, pull one stroke with the brush fanned to the left. Pull a second stroke that begins along the same point and fan this stroke to the right.

5] Pull and slightly taper the end. Both strokes join along their flat sides.

The front petal of these violets is created by painting two pointed pressure strokes that are each flat on one side. See pages 104-121 for the complete project.

Wiggly Pointed
Pressure Stroke

1] Pull a point. Then press and begin to curve the path.

2] Keep the pressure down as you pull and quickly curve in the opposite direction. This forms a wiggle in the middle of the stroke.

Comma Strokes

The comma stroke starts with pressure, similar to a pressure stroke. Then it gradually tapers to a sharp point. You can vary the stroke with a subtle or exaggerated curve.

Straight Comma Stroke

1. Press the brush to the surface. Pause to open the bristles.

2. Pull and immediately begin to gradually release pressure.

3. If required, pivot the brush slightly to begin the tail.

4. Continue to pull and taper the tail to a fine point.

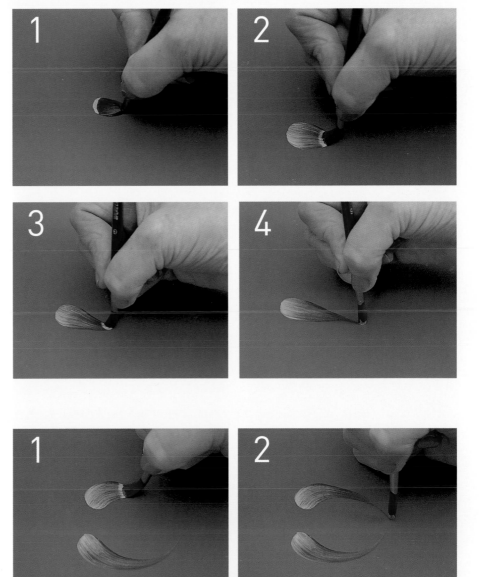

Curved Comma Stroke

1. Press the brush, beginning the curve (in this case to the right), as you continue to pull and release pressure.

2. Complete the curve and taper the tail to a fine point. There is no need to pivot the brush to form a tail in the curved comma.

Very Curved Comma

1] Press the brush to the surface.

2] Pull and begin to curve while releasing pressure.

3] Continue the curve.

4] Pull out the long tail, completing the curve.

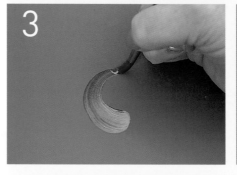

Very Curved Comma in the Opposite Direction

1] Press the brush to the surface, noting the angle of the brush and hand.

2] Pull and curve the stroke around.

3] Form the long tail, completing the curve.

Straight Fanned Comma Stroke

1. Lay the brush down with the ferrule resting on the surface.

2. Fan the brush open by gently twisting the brush from side to side in small increments.

3. Pull the brush, releasing pressure and pivoting the bristles slightly to begin the tail.

4. Continue to pull and taper the straight tail to a fine point.

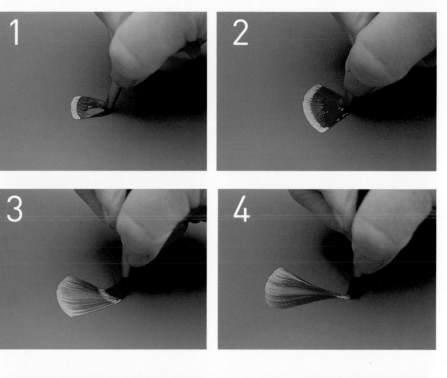

Curved Fanned Comma Stroke

1. Set the brush down with the ferrule resting on the surface. Fan the bristles open as in the straight fanned comma. Begin to pull in a curved path, releasing pressure.

2. Without pivoting, continue to pull and taper the curved tail to a fine point.

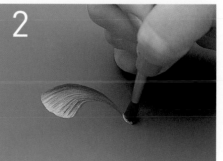

Troubleshooting

If your strokes lack the desired soft streaks, the problem may be your brush size. This tipping technique achieves soft streaks only when the brush is pressed firmly to the surface. The tipping color dominates the stroke on the left, done with a no. 6 round without pressure. The same size stroke on the right, done with a no. 2 round with pressure, shows the desired streaked effect.

Pointed Comma Strokes

The pointed comma stroke is perfect for many petals, leaves and turned edges. It starts and finishes with a point and can be modified with curves and wiggles.

Short Pointed Comma Stroke

1 Begin by pulling a point.

2 Gradually apply pressure while pulling the brush.

3 Then gradually release pressure to taper the stroke.

4 Continue to pull and taper the straight tail to a fine point. With larger brushes you may need to slightly pivot the brush.

The leaf directly under the right tulip is made with a pointed comma stroke. See pages 44–59 for the complete project.

Curved Pointed Comma

¹⟩ Begin by pulling a point.

²⟩ Gradually apply pressure while pulling the brush in a curved path, in this case to the left.

³⟩ Gradually release pressure to taper the stroke and pull out the tail.

⁴⟩ Here the curved pointed comma to the right is complete.

Troubleshooting

To refine the point at the top, load the liner with the tipping color. First tidy the edge on one side.

Repeat on the other side and continue the tip into a finer point.

To refine the tail, brush-mix the tail color, using the loading color plus the tipping color. Then tidy the sides and extend the tail into a fine point.

Wiggly Pointed Comma

1. Begin by pulling a point. As you continue to pull, gradually apply pressure and fan the bristles one way.

2. Then fan the bristles in the other direction.

3. Gradually release pressure to taper the stroke.

4. Continue to pull and slide on the brush tip to make the tail.

 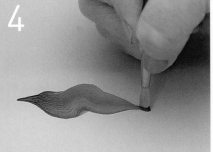

Long Pointed Comma with Quick Pressure

1. Pull a long curved point with the tip of the brush.

2. Stop pulling and apply quick pressure.

3. Pull the brush, gradually releasing pressure to taper the stroke. Slide on the brush tip to make the tail.

Short Pointed Comma with Quick Pressure

1 Use the no. 4 philbert for this stroke because its shape is short, wide and pointed. Pull a very short point.

2 Press the brush flat down with the ferrule resting on the surface. Open the bristles by gently twisting the brush from side to side in small increments.

3 Pull in a curved path, in this case to the right, while you release pressure to taper the stroke and pull out the tail.

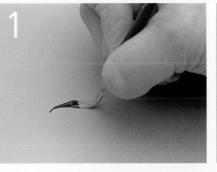

Wavy Pointed Comma with Long Tail

1 Use the no. 5 toler for this stroke because of its longer point and body. Pull a long point and gradually apply pressure in a curved path to the right.

2 Keep applying pressure as you change the direction of the path to the left.

3 Change the path direction back to the right, releasing pressure to taper the stroke into a long thin tail.

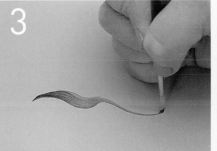

The long sepal on this columbine bud is made with a wavy pointed comma stroke with a long tail. See pages 92-103 for the complete project.

Straight Pointed Comma Flat on One Side

1 Pull a point, then press the brush firmly on the surface. Fan the bristles out to the left.

2 Pull the stroke, releasing pressure while keeping the right side of the stroke straight.

3 Slide on the brush tip to make the tail.

4 Turn the surface so you will see the tail of the first stroke while you do the second stroke. Beginning along the same point as the first, apply pressure and fan the bristles out to the right.

5 Pull the brush, releasing pressure. Keep the left side of the stroke straight as you taper and join it onto the tail of the first stroke. Two strokes are joined along the flat side. Note that left-handed painters would do the right side first.

The leaves of these cluster flowers start out as straight pointed comma strokes that are flat on one side. Then strokes are added to create the turned edges. See page 72–91 for the complete project.

More Strokes

Fan Stroke

[1] Press the brush down with the ferrule resting on the surface.

[2] Fan the brush open by gently twisting the brush from side to side in small increments.

[3] Push the brush forward slightly. The brush will fan out even more.

[4] Pull the brush down, toward you, releasing pressure. The brush tip will relax to a chisel.

[5] For a straight tail, pivot the bristles slightly.

[6] Slide on the chisel to form the tail.

[7] For a curved stroke, relax on the chisel.

[8] Slide on the chisel to form the tail.

[9] You can curve the stroke the other way too!

Teardrop Stroke

1] This stroke is shown with the no. 4 round, but a toler works well too. Pull a point. Begin to gradually apply pressure.

2] Continue to pull the brush, applying more pressure. Stop when the stroke is the desired length.

3] Relax the brush back onto its tip. Pull the tip three-fourths of the way through the stroke. Then lift straight up and off the surface.

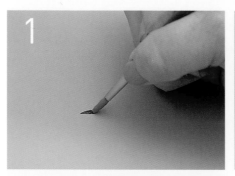

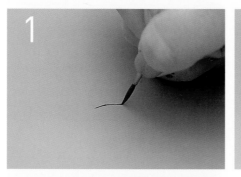

Hatpin Stroke

1] Fully load the liner and clean paint off the tip to make a sharp point. Pull a long line.

2] Press the tip down to make a small teardrop.

3] Relax back onto the tip and lift the brush off the surface.

Contour Stroke

1] Start with a thin line.

2] Press more on the curve to widen the line.

3] Release pressure to finish with a thin line. This stroke is often used to outline another stroke for added dimension.

4] Here are other examples of the contour stroke.

The front bluebell petals are lined with a contour stroke. See pages 72–91 for the complete project.

Common Mistakes

When one is first attempting brushstrokes, there is so much to learn—how to load and hold the brush and how to do the mechanical action involved in each different stroke. There are bound to be mistakes in the learning phase, and the resulting brushstrokes tell us the causes of the errors. Often there can be more than one cause, so be sure to check the entire list when trying to discover the reason for your less-than-perfect stroke. Although illustrated with comma strokes, the following errors are common in a variety of brushstrokes.

RIDGES ON BOTH SIDES OF THE STROKE

•The paint could be too thin. Perhaps you've added too much extender to the paint puddle, or you forgot to shake the bottle before pouring paint on the palette.
•You may have failed to get all the water out of your brush before loading in paint.

•Perhaps you've pulled too much paint into the brush. Check the loading zone on your palette to see if there is texture there, as this indicates that there is too much paint in the brush.

A LARGE RIDGE ON JUST ONE SIDE OF THE STROKE

This is a sign that you are holding the handle off to one side. This pulls the tip of the brush along the far side of the stroke rather than up the center of it. If you're right-handed, the puddle is probably on the right side with the point of the brush being pulled along the left side of the stroke. If you're left-handed, the effect is probably reversed.

SPLIT TAIL AT THE END OF THE STROKE

•You may be doing the stroke too fast, so the brush doesn't relax back up to its tip.
•The paint could be too thick. Try adding another drop of extender to the puddle.
•Did you forget to dampen the brush before loading in paint? This results in uneven paint distribution within the brush.
•You may not be reloading often enough. With this technique, you usually reload for every stroke.

•You may not have loaded the brush all the way to the ferrule, which is required for the brush to spring back to form the tail of the stroke.
•You may not have worked paint into the center of the brush, resulting in dry pockets.
•The brush may be worn out or one not designed for strokework.

BLOB OF COLOR IN THE TAIL OF THE STROKE

•You may have twisted the brush at the end of the stroke too much, which propels any remaining paint off the tip. Slow down as you pull the stroke. If the brush relaxes back up to a chisel rather than a point, just twist a little to allow you to form the tail by sliding on the chisel.

•You may have lifted the brush straight up and off at the end of the stroke rather than sweeping into the "follow through" phase.
•The paint could be too thin. Perhaps you've added too much extender to the paint puddle, or you forgot to shake the bottle before pouring paint on the palette.
•Did you remember to get all the water out of your brush before loading in paint?

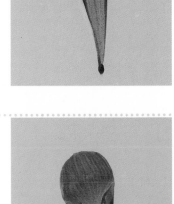

SQUARE STROKE

You've laid the brush down with pressure. Then without moving the brush, you abruptly released pressure and relaxed the brush back up to its tip, which is still at the top of the stroke. The tip was then dragged

through the deposit of paint. To prevent this error, do not start releasing pressure until the brush begins to move along the path of the stroke.

POINT ON THE HEAD OF A COMMA STROKE

•When laying the brush down, you may have pushed forward.
•Check the position of the handle in the approach phase. If it is perpendicular to the surface, move it back slightly to point at your forehead.
•You forgot to pause at the beginning to allow the brush to open before pulling the brush along its path.

•You may be rolling the brush when you load it, forming a sharp point on the brush.
•There may be an extra long hair in the brush that should be pulled out or carefully trimmed.

Fixing Mistakes

Here are my tips for fixing your less-than-perfect strokes right on your surface. There's no need to wipe them off and start over.

PROBLEM

Not enough tipping color In this stroke, there's not enough tipping color to streak through the whole stroke.

SOLUTION

Thin the tipping color with extra extender. Use the liner to pull many fine lines of varying lengths down from the tip into the body of the stroke.

Brush mix loading color plus tipping color for fine lines in the midsection of the stroke.

PROBLEM

Too much tipping color In this stroke, the tipping color dominates the stroke.

SOLUTION

Thin the loading color with extra extender. Pull many fine lines up from the tail into the body of the stroke. Vary the length of the lines.

Brush mix the tipping color plus loading color for fine lines in the midsection of the stroke.

PROBLEM

Head of comma stoke is not round
This comma stroke has an imperfect head.

SOLUTION

Cover over the flaw and reshape the head of the comma with the background color.

PROBLEM

The tail is too wide This comma stroke has a thick tail that does not taper to a point.

SOLUTION 1

Reshape the tail using the background color. Start along the body of the stroke and create a smooth taper on one side, covering over the wide part of the tail.

Repeat on the other side of the tail to form a fine point.

SOLUTION 2

Brush mix the loading color plus tipping color on the liner to make the same color seen in the tail. Begin a line along the side of the body and use it to extend the tail further on one side.

Repeat on the other side, bringing the line down to meet the other to form a clean, sharp tail.

Heart Basket
with Beginner Roses & Tulips

You've learned the strokes and now you are ready to put those newfound skills to work. This project is the perfect one to start with, as it uses so many of those brushstrokes. This charming wire basket would be at home in any room. I hope that once you've painted it you will be inspired to go on to the next project, which uses the same flowers in a different color scheme and pattern. To see other ways these flowers might be used, look at the counter cubby and the platter in the Gallery of Ideas, pages 122-125.

SURFACE

Heart box, item 232002, from Painters Paradise
(See Resources on page 126.)

MAUREEN MCNAUGHTON BRUSHES

no. 4 round, no. 6 round, no. 00 liner,
1-inch (25mm) basecoat/varnish flat

ADDITIONAL SUPPLIES

extender: water + DecoArt Easy Float (3:1), light transfer paper,
regular cotton swabs, Krylon Silver Leafing Pen, DecoArt DuraClear Satin Varnish

Palette

DecoArt Americana Acrylic Paints *indicates colors that DO NOT require extender*

French Grey Blue (Background Color)

Pineapple

Moon Yellow

Camel

Reindeer Moss Green

Light Avocado

Avocado

dv. Green: Black Green + Avocado (1:1)

*Midnite Green

Black Green

Mint Julep Green

Green Mist

Arbor Green

*Deep Teal

Hauser Dark Green

*Payne's Grey

Orchid

mv. Violet: Orchid + Pansy Lavender (1:1)

Pansy Lavender

Plum

Baby Pink

French Mauve

mv. Red Violet: French Mauve + Antique Mauve (1:1)

Mauve

*Antique Mauve

*Cranberry Wine

*Red Violet

This pattern may be hand-traced or photo-copied for personal use only. Enlarge at 134 percent to bring up to full size. Solid-head arrows indicate pointed comma strokes. Blunt-head arrows indicate comma strokes.

Surface Preparation & Rose Leaves

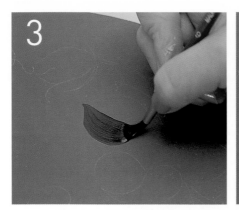

Surface Preparation

step 1 Prepare the surface with French Grey Blue as instructed on pages 10-11.

step 2 When the surface is dry, trace on the pattern with light-colored transfer paper as instructed on page 12.

Rose Leaves

step 3 Load the no. 6 round in Midnite Green and tip in Avocado. On one half of each warm rose leaf (marked "warm" on the pattern), pull a pointed pressure stroke fanned on one side and flat on the other. Start at the leaf tip and pull into the rose.

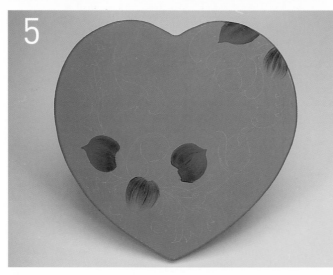

step 4 Reload the brush and repeat the stroke on the other side of the leaf.

step 5 Paint the remaining two warm rose leaves this same way. Load the no. 6 round in Midnite Green and tip in Arbor Green for the two cool rose leaves.

step 6 Load the no. 4 round in Light Avocado and tip in Reindeer Moss Green. Pull a pointed comma with a long point and quick pressure to form a turned edge on one side of the warm leaf. Turn the surface as needed to make stroking easier.

step 7 | Pull an S-shaped pointed comma on the other side of the leaf.

step 8 | Join a shorter comma stroke inside the curve of the previous stroke to complete the turn on this side of the leaf.

step 9 | Load the no. 00 liner with the tipping color, in this case Reindeer Moss Green, and extend the light points into sharper points.

step 10 | Repeat to form the turned edges on all warm rose leaves. Load the no. 4 round in Green Mist and tip in Mint Julep Green for the turned edges on the cool rose leaves. Refer to the photograph for placement.

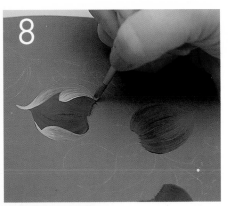

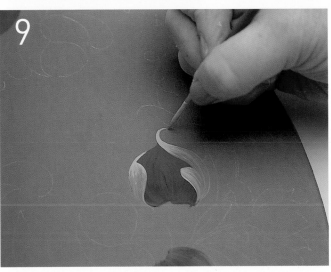

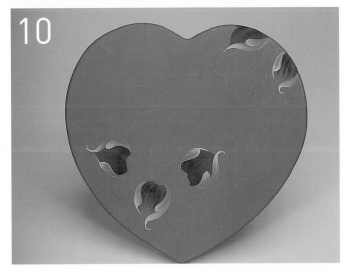

Tulip Leaves & Roses

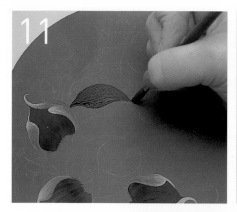

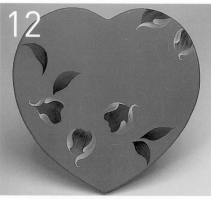

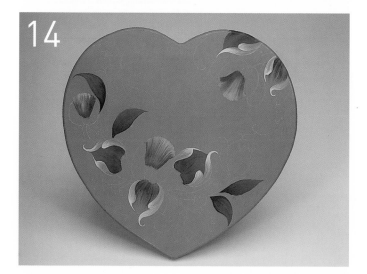

Tulip Leaves

step 11] Load the no. 6 round in Deep Teal and tip in Hauser Dark Green for the cool tulip leaves (marked "cool" on the pattern). Pull a pointed comma stroke out from the stem over the traced arrow, centering the stroke on the arrow.

step 12] Pull in the remaining cool tulip leaf the same way. Load the no. 6 round in Avocado and tip in Black Green to paint the two warm tulip leaves.

Roses

step 13] Load the no. 6 round in Red Violet and tip in mv. Violet. Pull a fan stroke to form the opening in the rose. Begin the stroke slightly inside the opening with the brush on the dotted line. Fan the brush open to meet the sides of the opening. Push out to the edge of the opening. Then pull down into the bowl petals.

step 14] Repeat the same fan stroke in the opening of the remaining two roses.

step 15 Load the no. 6 round in Red Violet and tip in Orchid for the lighter side petals. Form the first light petal by pulling a comma stroke back to the bowl.

step 16 Pull in another light petal on the other side of the bowl of the large rose. Then paint one comma stroke around the bowl of the medium rose. Load the no. 6 round in Red Violet and tip in mv. Violet. With these colors, pull a third comma stroke on the large rose. Reload the brush with Red Violet tipped in mv. Violet, and paint the comma stroke on the other side of the medium rose.

step 17 Load the no. 00 liner in Payne's Grey to shade the strokes in the rose. Pull fine lines of various lengths up from the base of the fan stroke and up from the point of the comma stroke petals.

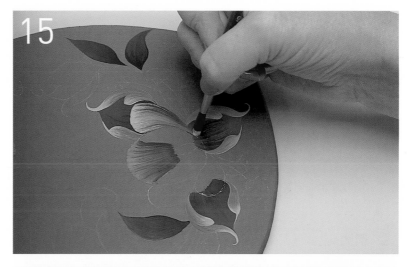

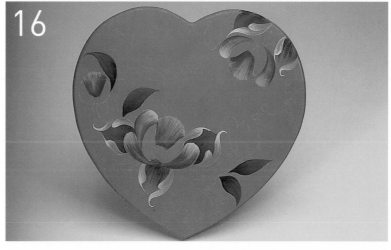

Roses, continued

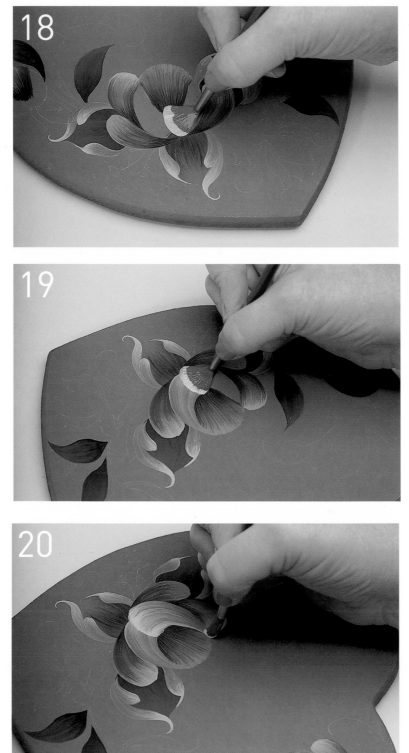

step 18 Form the outer bowl of the rose with two fanned comma strokes. Load the no. 6 round in Pansy Lavender and tip in Orchid for the darker stroke. Start the stroke in the middle of the bowl. Fan it open to fill in the depth of the bowl.

step 19 Wrap the tail around the fan stroke to complete the stroke. When the dark stroke is dry, load the no. 6 round in Pansy Lavender and tip in Baby Pink. Start this stroke on the head of the previous stroke.

step 20 Wrap the tail around the fan stroke to complete the circular-shaped opening. If the dark stroke shows through this lighter stroke, apply a second application.

step 21] With these same colors, paint the fanned comma strokes to form the bowl of the bud and the medium rose. Load the no. 00 liner with Orchid. Line the smooth edge of the opening. Line the ragged edge of the fan stroke with a broken line. Repeat for each of the roses.

step 22] Load the no. 00 liner with Camel. Highlight the opening again with a line, but this time, place the color only where the line turns from front to back.

step 23] Load the liner with Antique Mauve. Pull fine lines of varying lengths from the point down into the body of the two bowl strokes.

step 24] With the liner, stipple pollen dots at the base of the opening of each rose. First stipple with Avocado and then add a few with Light Avocado. Finish with a few dots of Moon Yellow.

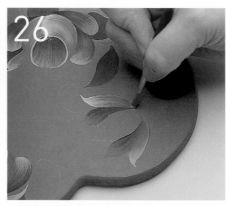

step 25 Load the no. 4 round with Cranberry Wine and tip in Mauve. Form the rear petals with a pointed comma stroke pulled down from the tip of each dark rear petal.

step 26 Load the no. 4 round with Antique Mauve and tip in French Mauve. Pull a pointed comma down to the stem to form the side petals. The side petal will overlap the adjacent rear petal.

step 27 Pull in the rear and side petals on all tulips.

step 28 Intensify the shading in the dark point of the rear petals. Load the no. 00 liner in Red Violet. Pull lines of varying length into the body of the stroke.

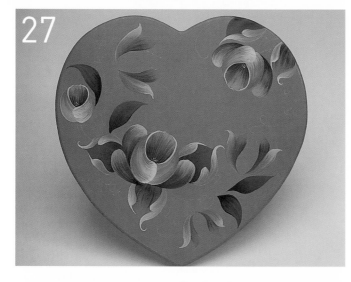

step 29 Load the no. 4 round with French Mauve and tip in Antique Mauve. Pull a pointed comma stroke, fanned on the outer edge and flat on the inside edge, from the tip down to the stem to form half of the center petal. Repeat on all the tulips.

step 30 Form the other half of the center petal with the same stroke. Repeat these two strokes on all tulips.

step 31 Refine the points on all petals with the tipping color used in the stroke. Load the no. 00 liner with Pineapple. Pull fine lines of varying lengths up from the base of each middle tulip petal.

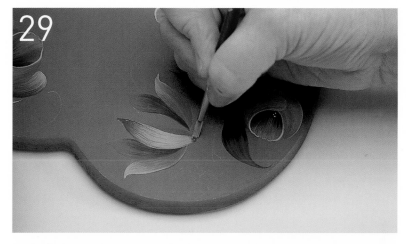

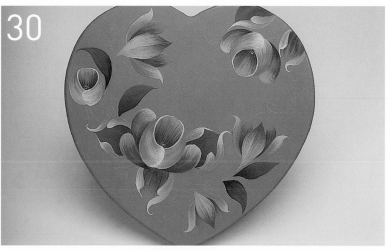

Details & Finishing

step 32 | Load the no. 00 liner with Mauve. Pull a center vein in each rose leaf. Start at the rose and taper the line at the end. This repeats the tulip color near the roses and helps to tie all the elements together.

step 33 | In the same way, pull a vein in each tulip leaf with Pansy Lavender. This repeats the rose color by the tulips.

step 34 | Load the no. 4 round with Arbor Green and tip in Hauser Dark Green. Pull pointed comma strokes down from the base of the small- and medium-size roses to form the sepals.

step 35 | Load the no. 00 liner with Light Avocado. Pull fine lines of varying lengths from the stem up into the yellow base of the tulip petals. Let the yellow and green weave together.

step 36 | With Avocado loaded on the liner, pull in the rest of the tulip stem, merging the two greens together. Pull in the rose stems with the same color and brush.

step 37 Load the liner with dv. Green. Shade the stems with lines where they come out from under another object. Highlight some sections of the stems with a line of Reindeer Moss Green.

step 38 Load the liner with Pansy Lavender. Pull in the tendrils and the stems to the fluffies. Highlight some of the tendrils with a line of mv. Violet.

step 39 Repeat the rose colors on the fluffies near the tulips. Stipple Pansy Lavender on the heads of all violet fluffies with the regular cotton swab. Then lightly stipple mv. Violet over the entire head. Allow the darker color underneath to show through.

step 40 Finish with the mv. Violet. Then stipple Camel very lightly on one side of each fluffy as a highlight.

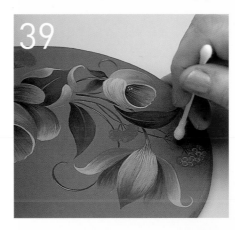

Details & Finishing, continued

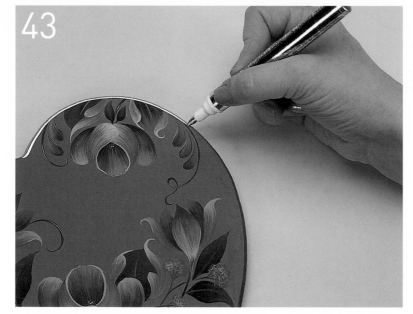

step 41 Use pinks from the tulips to paint the fluffies under the rose. Use the cotton swabs to stipple these fluffies with Antique Mauve, then with mv. Red Violet and finishing with Camel.

step 42 Fill in the nooks and crannies of the design with loose comma strokes. Use the no. 4 round loaded with mv. Violet and tipped in Plum.

step 43 Rest the wide edge of the Krylon Silver Leafing Pen on the rim of the heart. Run it all along the edge to form a neat border. Use the same pen to fill in the side of the lid.

Erase any visible transfer lines. When the silver leafing is thoroughly dry, apply several coats of DecoArt DuraClear Satin Varnish to both sides of the lid with the 1-inch (25mm) basecoat/varnish brush.

Completed Heart Basket

Top View

Side View

Floral Corner Shelf
with Faux Finish & Leafing

Everyone can use an extra shelf in the home or office. You might use this one to showcase your favorite plant or perhaps a family photo.

In the palette for this project, you are pairing two sets of complements. Complements are colors that fall directly opposite each other on the color wheel. In this project the complements are yellow and violet, and red and green. Pairing complements in this way creates excitement in your painting. This project also introduces a faux finish and the application of gold leaf. Both techniques are easy to do and lend an elegant touch.

SURFACE

Corner shelf, item 8878, from Walnut Hollow (See Resources on page 126.)

MAUREEN MCNAUGHTON BRUSHES

no. 4 round, no. 6 round, no. 5 toler, no. 00 liner,
1-inch (25mm) basecoat/varnish flat, 2-inch (51mm) flat

ADDITIONAL SUPPLIES

extender: water + DecoArt Easy Float (3:1), plastic wrap, chalk pencil, ruler, Bondo spreader or eraser, Scotch Magic Tape, gold leaf adhesive, old brush (for applying gold leaf adhesive), gold leaf, velvet cloth, light transfer paper, regular cotton swabs, DecoArt DuraClear Satin Varnish

Palette

DecoArt Americana Acrylic Paints: DM = DecoArt Dazzling Metallics, RM = DecoArt Royal Metallics
indicates colors that DO NOT require extender

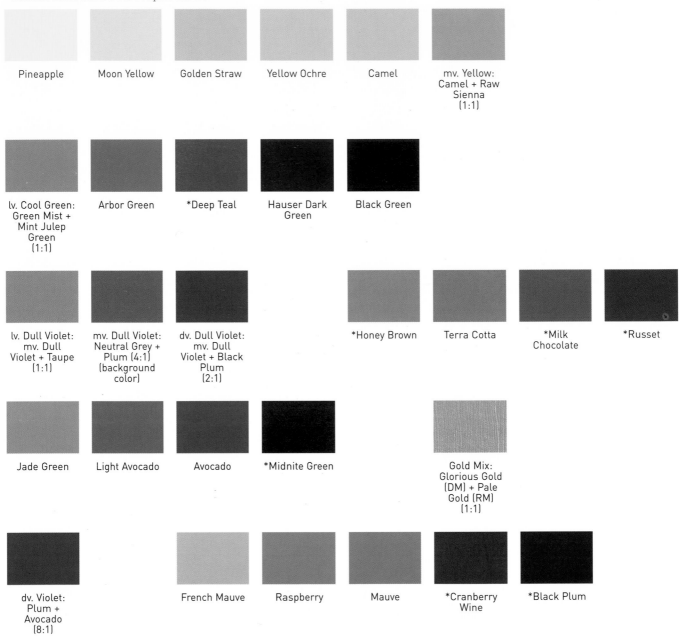

Pineapple

Moon Yellow

Golden Straw

Yellow Ochre

Camel

mv. Yellow:
Camel + Raw
Sienna
(1:1)

lv. Cool Green:
Green Mist +
Mint Julep
Green
(1:1)

Arbor Green

*Deep Teal

Hauser Dark
Green

Black Green

lv. Dull Violet:
mv. Dull
Violet + Taupe
(1:1)

mv. Dull Violet:
Neutral Grey +
Plum (4:1)
(background
color)

dv. Dull Violet:
mv. Dull
Violet + Black
Plum
(2:1)

*Honey Brown

Terra Cotta

*Milk
Chocolate

*Russet

Jade Green

Light Avocado

Avocado

*Midnite Green

Gold Mix:
Glorious Gold
(DM) + Pale
Gold (RM)
(1:1)

dv. Violet:
Plum +
Avocado
(8:1)

French Mauve

Raspberry

Mauve

*Cranberry
Wine

*Black Plum

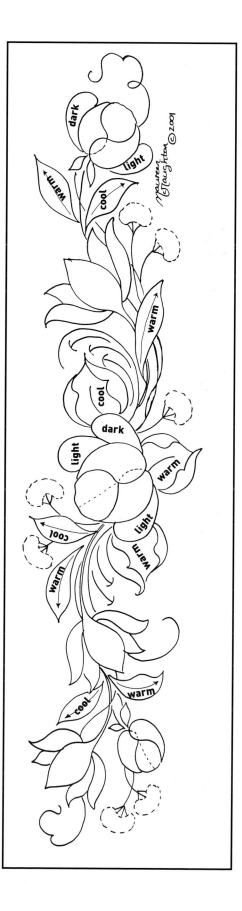

These patterns may be hand-traced or photo-copied for personal use only. Enlarge at 189 percent to bring up to full size.

On the rose and tulip pattern, the solid-head arrows indicate pointed comma strokes. The blunt-head arrows indicate comma strokes.

Faux Finish

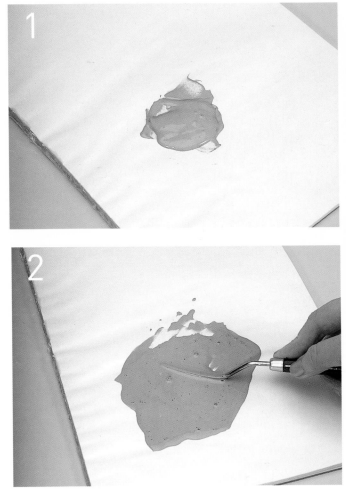

step 1 | Prepare the surface as described under Surface Preparation on pages 10-11. Basecoat the surface with mv. Dull Violet. Place a large puddle of lv. Dull Violet on the palette.

step 2 | Use the palette knife to mix lv. Dull Violet and extender (2:1) to make a watery consistency.

step 3 | Brush on a generous coat of extender with the 2-inch (51mm) flat, using pressure to push the extender into the surface.

step 4 | Quickly apply the diluted lv. Dull Violet mix over the wet surface with the 2-inch (51mm) flat. This coat must cover the entire area but does not need to be neat.

step 5 Loosely place plastic wrap over the wet paint. Begin to smoosh the wrap with your fingers.

step 6 Push and twist the wrap with your hands to create more wrinkles for added texture.

step 7 Remove the plastic wrap. Any bubbles will disappear as the paint dries. If you don't like the result, immediately dampen the surface with more extender and paint, and repeat the process. Allow this to dry thoroughly.

Gold Leafing

step 8 Measure 1¼" (32mm) from the edge of the long side and mark the line with a chalk pencil and ruler. Place tape on the outside of this line. Burnish the taped edge by dragging the Bondo spreader or an eraser along it. This prevents paint seepage under the tape.

step 9 Basecoat the area from the tape to the front of the shelf, including the edge, with dv. Dull Violet.

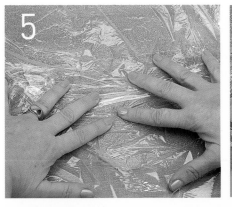

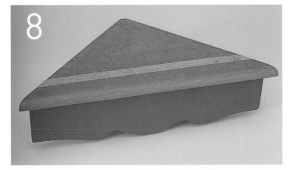

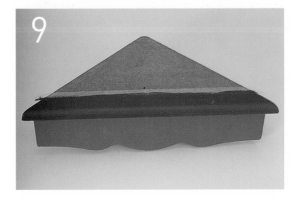

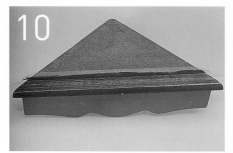

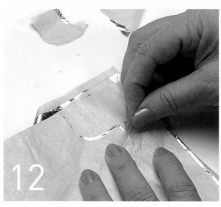

step 10 When dry, chalk the lines for the narrow gold band beside the faux finish and the wider gold band along the shelf's front edge. Use a ruler to make the lines straight. Apply tape along both lines and burnish the edges.

step 11 Use an old brush to apply gold leaf adhesive in the narrow and wide bands. Immediately remove the tape. Allow the adhesive to dry for the time indicated in the label instructions.

step 12 Tear the leafing and the tissue paper covering it into small pieces. Keeping the paper on the leafing helps to make sure the same side of the leafing is used on the entire project. It also reduces the chances of tarnishing caused from handling the leafing.

step 13 Place the pieces of gold leaf over the adhesive, overlapping the edges. Then remove the tissue paper.

step 14 After covering the entire band with gold leaf, burnish it with a velvet cloth to remove excess.

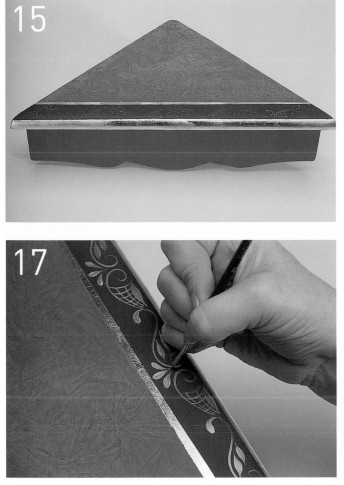

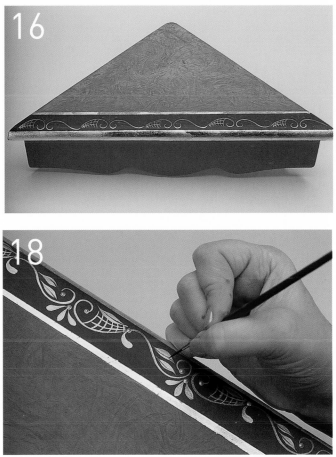

step 15 | Transfer the pattern for the strokework border with light transfer paper.

step 16 | Mix equal parts of Pale Gold and Glorious Gold. Load the no. 00 liner in this gold mix and pull in all linework.

step 17 | Load the no. 5 toler in the Gold Mix and pull in the pointed comma and comma strokes.

step 18 | Use the end of the brush handle to make the gold dots. When the dots are dry, pull veins in each pointed comma leaf with Black Plum. To prevent tarnishing the gold leaf, apply one coat of varnish to the top of the shelf and the gold leaf.

Rose & Tulip Leaves

Rose Leaves

Tulip Leaves

Rose Leaves

step 19 Trace on the pattern with light-colored transfer paper. Note that the painting order and the brush strokes are generally the same as shown in the step-by-step photos for the heart basket on pages 44-59.

step 20 Load the no. 6 round in Midnite Green and tip in Light Avocado. Pull a pointed pressure stroke, fanned on one side and flat on the other, on one half of a warm rose leaf (marked "warm" on the pattern). Start at the leaf tip and pull into the rose. Reload the brush and repeat the stroke on the other side of the leaf. Paint the remaining two warm rose leaves this same way.

step 21 Load the no. 6 round in Hauser Dark Green and tip in Arbor Green for the two cool rose leaves (marked "cool" on the pattern).

step 22 Load the no. 4 round in Avocado and tip in Jade Green. Pull a pointed comma with a long point and quick pressure to form a turned edge on one side of the warm leaves. Pull an S-shaped pointed comma on the other side of the leaf. Join a shorter comma stroke inside the curve of the previous stroke to complete the turn on this side of the leaf.

step 23 Load the no. 4 round in Deep Teal and tip in lv. Cool Green for the turned edges on the cool rose leaves. Refer to the photograph for placement.

step 24 Load the no. 00 liner with the tipping color and extend the light points into sharper points.

Tulip Leaves

step 25 Load the no. 6 round in Deep Teal and tip in Black Green for the cool tulip leaves (marked "cool" on the pattern). Pull a pointed comma stroke over the traced arrow, centering the stroke on the arrow.

step 26 Load the no. 6 round in Avocado and tip in Black Green for the warm tulip leaves (marked "warm" on the pattern). Pull in pointed comma strokes as you did for the cool tulip leaves.

step 27 | Use the no. 6 round for the middle and right rose (see photo on the top left of page 68), and the no. 4 round for the smaller rose on the left (see photo at right). Load with Russet and tip in Honey Brown. Pull a fan stroke to form the opening in the roses. Begin the stroke slightly inside the opening with the brush on the dotted line. Fan the brush open to meet the sides of the opening. Push out to the edge of the opening. Then pull down into the bowl petals.

step 28 | Load the no. 6 round in Milk Chocolate and tip in Yellow Ochre for the two top side petals on the middle rose and the lower side petal on the right rose. (These light petals are marked on the pattern.) Form the petals by pulling a comma stroke back to the bowl.

step 29 | For each rose's third side petal (marked "dark" on the pattern), load the no. 6 round in Russet and tip in Honey Brown.

step 30 | Load the no. 00 liner in Russet to shade the strokes in the roses. Pull fine lines of various lengths up from the base of the fan-stroke petals and up from the point of the comma-stroke petals. Repeat with shorter lines of Black Plum.

step 31 | Form the outer bowl of the rose with two fanned comma strokes. Load the no. 6 round in Terra Cotta and tip in Golden Straw for the darker stroke. Start the stroke in the middle of the bowl. Fan it open to fill in the depth of the bowl. Wrap the tail around the fan stroke.

step 32 | When the dark stroke is dry, load the no. 6 round in Terra Cotta and tip in Moon Yellow. Start this stroke on the head of the previous stroke. Wrap the tail around the fan stroke to complete the circular-shaped opening. If the dark stroke shows through this lighter stroke, apply a second application.

step 33 | Load the no. 00 liner with Golden Straw. Line the smooth edge of the opening. Line the ragged edge of the fan stroke with a broken line.

step 34 | Load the no. 00 liner with Pineapple. Highlight the opening again with a line, just where it turns from front to back.

step 35 | Load the no. 00 liner with a brush mix of Raspberry + Cranberry Wine. On the darker bowl petal only, pull fine lines of varying lengths from the point down into the body of the stroke to repeat the tulip color.

step 36 | Stipple pollen dots at the base of the opening with the no. 00 liner. First stipple Avocado, then a few Light Avocado and finally three or four dots of Moon Yellow.

Tulips

step 37 (See above photo.) Load the no. 4 round with Cranberry Wine and tip in Terra Cotta. Form the rear petals on all tulips with a pointed comma stroke pulled down from the tip of each dark rear petal.

step 38 Load the no. 4 round with Raspberry and tip in mv. Yellow. Pull a pointed comma down to the stem to form the side petals. The side petal will overlap the adjacent rear petal.

step 39 Load the no. 00 liner with Cranberry Wine. Pull fine lines of varying lengths up from the point of the rear petals for shading.

step 40 For the center petal, use the no. 4 round for the small tulip on the left, and the no. 6 round for the remaining tulips. Load with Camel and tip in Raspberry. Pull a pointed comma stroke, fanned on the outer edge and flat on the inside edge, from the tip down to the stem to form half of the center petal. Form the other half of the center petal with the same stroke.

step 41 Use the no. 00 liner to refine the points on all petals with the tipping color used in the stroke.

step 42 Load the no. 00 liner with Moon Yellow. Pull fine lines of varying lengths up from the base of the middle petal. Then pull a few more lines with Pineapple.

Details

step 43 Load the no. 00 liner with Mauve. Start at the stem end of all rose and tulip leaves and pull in a center vein that tapers at the end.

step 44 Load the no. 4 round in Arbor Green and tip in Hauser Dark Green. Pull in the sepals on the right and left rose, with pointed commas pulled out from the flower.

step 45 Load the no. 00 liner with a brush mix of Light Avocado and Jade Green. It must be lighter than the mv. Dull Violet background. Pull in the rose and tulip stems. Pull fine lines of varying lengths from the stem up into the yellow base of the tulip petals. Let the yellow and green weave together.

step 46 Pull in the tendrils and the stems to the fluffy flowers with dv. Violet. Shade where they come out from under an object with a brush mix of Plum + Black Green. Highlight with a brush mix of French Mauve + Mauve.

Fluffies

step 47 (See photo above.) Stipple dv. Violet on the heads of all fluffies with the regular cotton swab. Then lightly stipple Mauve over the entire head. Allow the darker color underneath to show through.

step 48 Highlight one side of each fluffy by lightly stippling French Mauve.

Commas

step 49 (See above photo.) Loose comma strokes fill in nooks and crannies of the design. Load the no. 4 round with dv. Violet and tip in Raspberry.

Finishing

step 50 Erase any visible transfer lines. Apply several coats of DecoArt DuraClear Satin Varnish to all shelf surfaces with the 1-inch (25mm) basecoat/varnish brush.

Completed Corner Shelf

Side View

Top View

Floral Memory Album
with Faux Finish & Lettering

This memory album is the perfect home for our treasured photos of moments captured in time. See how the bumble bees fly lazily from one flower to the next, spreading touches of sunny yellow throughout the painting, while the ladybug climbs the stem of the Johnny-jump-up, bringing a touch of deep orange to that corner. The delicate wings of a butterfly carry a touch of blue from the bluebells up to the narcissus, and the same blue is repeated with tendrils wrapped around the lily and cluster flower stems. This repetition of color unites the floral vignettes and creates both color and composition harmony in the painting.

SURFACE

Contemporary memory album cover, item 3700, from Walnut Hollow
(See Resources on page 126.)

MAUREEN MCNAUGHTON BRUSHES

no. 2 round, no. 4 round, no. 6 round, no. 5 toler, no. 9 toler, no. 00 liner,
no. 4 philbert, no. 1 mop, no. 6 flat, no. 10 flat, 2-inch (51mm) flat

ADDITIONAL SUPPLIES

extender: water + DecoArt Easy Float (3:1), light transfer paper,
regular cotton swabs, pointed cotton swabs, Scotch Magic Tape, craft knife,
ruler, Bondo spreader, rubbing alcohol, toothbrush, plastic wrap,
stylus tool, DecoArt DuraClear Satin Varnish

Palette

DecoArt Americana Acrylic Paints *indicates colors that DO NOT require extender*

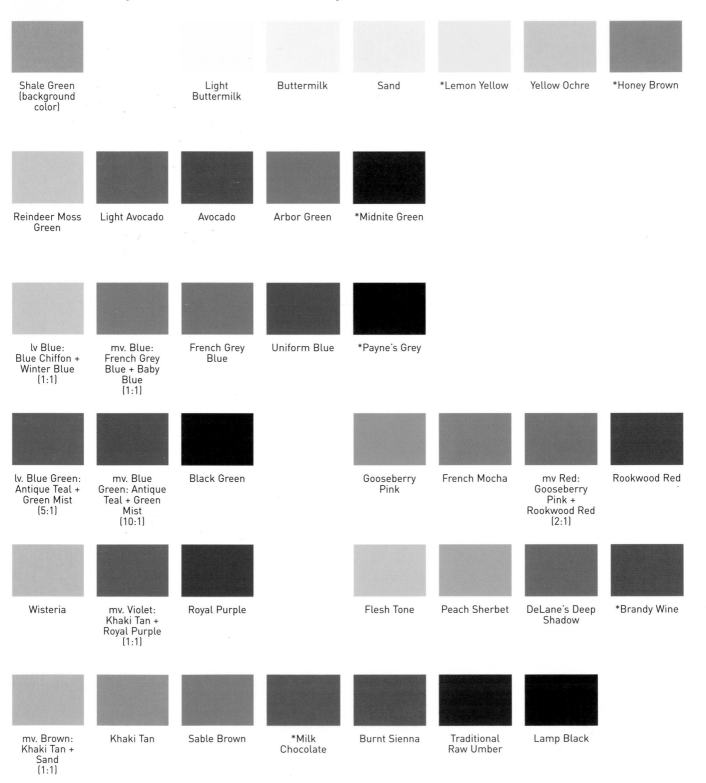

Shale Green (background color)   **Light Buttermilk**   **Buttermilk**   **Sand**   ***Lemon Yellow**   **Yellow Ochre**   ***Honey Brown**

Reindeer Moss Green   **Light Avocado**   **Avocado**   **Arbor Green**   ***Midnite Green**

lv Blue: Blue Chiffon + Winter Blue (1:1)   **mv. Blue: French Grey Blue + Baby Blue (1:1)**   **French Grey Blue**   **Uniform Blue**   ***Payne's Grey**

lv. Blue Green: Antique Teal + Green Mist (5:1)   **mv. Blue Green: Antique Teal + Green Mist (10:1)**   **Black Green**   **Gooseberry Pink**   **French Mocha**   **mv Red: Gooseberry Pink + Rookwood Red (2:1)**   **Rookwood Red**

Wisteria   **mv. Violet: Khaki Tan + Royal Purple (1:1)**   **Royal Purple**   **Flesh Tone**   **Peach Sherbet**   **DeLane's Deep Shadow**   ***Brandy Wine**

mv. Brown: Khaki Tan + Sand (1:1)   **Khaki Tan**   **Sable Brown**   ***Milk Chocolate**   **Burnt Sienna**   **Traditional Raw Umber**   **Lamp Black**

This pattern may be hand-traced or photocopied for personal use only. Enlarge at 143 percent to bring up to full size.

Surface Preparation & Faux Finish

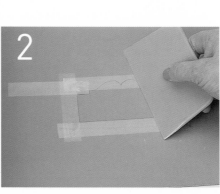

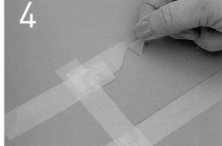

Surface Preparation

step 1] Remove the hardware and basecoat the cover of the album with Shale Green. Transfer the pattern onto the album cover with light transfer paper. Use a ruler to keep the lines straight on the lettering panel.

step 2] Tape around the straight edges of the panel and tape over the scalloped area. Burnish the tape with the Bondo spreader.

step 3] Use the craft knife to carefully cut through the tape around the scallops.

step 4] Pull away the tape inside the panel. Protect the area outside of the panel with paper.

Faux Finish

step 5] Do the following faux finish in the panel, on the small hinged section, on the back cover and on the back of the front cover. Basecoat the surfaces with mv. Blue Green. Do the smooshed plastic technique described on pages 64-65 with Black Green. Allow this to dry.

step 6] On the palette, mix lv. Blue Green with extender (2:1) to make it a watery consistency. Brush additional extender on the surface. Crumple a piece of plastic wrap and tap it in the paint. Pounce out the excess on the palette until you see an open pattern.

step 7] Tap the color over the entire wet surface.

step 8] While the paint is still wet, spatter rubbing alcohol over the surface with a stiff toothbrush to create a lacy effect. Remove the remaining tape around the inset panel.

step 9 | Load the no. 4 round in Royal Purple and tip in French Grey Blue. Pull tapered pressure strokes into the center for the top two petals on both flowers.

step 10 | Load the no. 4 round in French Grey Blue and tip in Wisteria. Pull tapered pressure strokes into the center for the side petals. Turn the surface to pull the strokes toward you.

step 11 | Load the no. 4 round in Sable Brown and tip in Yellow Ochre. Form the large yellow petal with two pressure strokes pulled into the center. Fan the strokes on the outer edge and keep the inner edges flat.

step 12 | Shade all the petals with fine lines of varying lengths pulled out from the flower center with the no. 00 liner. On the side petals use a brush mix of Royal Purple + French Grey Blue. On the top petals use Payne's Grey and on the yellow petal use Milk Chocolate.

step 13 | Use the no. 00 liner to paint the arc-shaped highlight in the top petals with fine lines of Wisteria. Then pull lines of Payne's Grey in the yellow petal.

step 14 | Fill in the oval in the center with Yellow Ochre. Dot Brandy Wine in the top of the oval. Load the no. 00 liner in Light Buttermilk. Frame the oval with small commas, extending the tails along the sides of the yellow petal.

step 15 | Load the no. 2 round with Reindeer Moss Green and tip in Avocado. Form the leaves with curved pressure strokes, pulling them from the outer edge to the middle vein. Start with the first stroke along the lower edge.

Johnny-jump-ups, continued & Ladybug

step 16 Continue to pull nesting pressure strokes, working up to the leaf tip. Pull a pointed pressure stroke at the tip.

step 17 Complete the other side of the leaf with nesting pressure strokes, starting with the lower stroke. Repeat for all leaves.

step 18 Load the no. 00 liner in Royal Purple. Pull in the leaf stem and center vein in each leaf. Load the liner with a brush mix of Yellow Ochre + Light Buttermilk. Halfway between the vein and the outer edge, pull many fine lines. This highlight indicates where the leaf bends.

Load the liner with Light Avocado and pull in the flower stems. Shade where they come out from the leaf or flower with lines, using a brush mix of Light Avocado + Midnite Green. Highlight some sections with a brush mix of Yellow Ochre + Light Buttermilk. Load the liner in mv. Blue and pull in the tendrils. Shade them with Uniform Blue and highlight with lv. Blue.

Ladybug

step 19 Fill in the ladybug shell with DeLane's Deep Shadow. Float Rookwood Red shading on the back end of the shell with the no. 6 flat. Use the same brush to float a highlight of Peach Sherbet on the head end of the shell.

step 20 Load the no. 00 liner with Traditional Raw Umber. Paint the head, spots and antennae.

step 21] Load the no. 2 round in Peach Sherbet and tip in DeLane's Deep Shadow. Pull a pointed comma stroke to form the turned edge of the lily petal.

step 22] With the same brush and colors, pull a pointed comma to create the other turned petal. Form the side petals on the buds with pointed commas pulled down to the stem. Paint the cone shape where the stem attaches to the large lily with a pointed comma pulled to the stem.

step 23] Load the no. 4 round with Yellow Ochre and tip in DeLane's Deep Shadow. Pull two pointed comma strokes back to the flower's center to form both of the petals with turned edges.

step 24] With the same brush and colors, pull a pointed comma for the remaining petals, pulling the strokes back to the flower center. Pull one pointed comma out from the stem for the center petals in the buds.

step 25] Refine petal tips with the no. 00 liner and the tipping color. Then load in Brandy Wine and line the turned edges where they turn from front to back. Darken the petal tips that cross over other petals with fine lines of Brandy Wine.

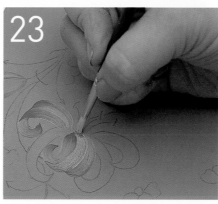

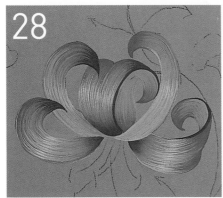

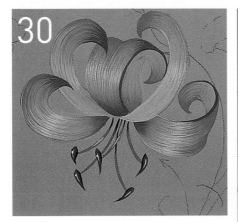

step 26 With the no. 10 flat, float DeLane's Deep Shadow shading on the base of the middle and outer petals.

step 27 Intensify the shading with a float of Brandy Wine at the base of the first application.

step 28 Load the no. 00 liner with Yellow Ochre. Pull lines in the middle section of each petal to cover any dark streaks that may be in the highlight area. Then highlight these same areas with fine lines, using a brush mix of Lemon Yellow + Light Buttermilk.

step 29 Load the no. 00 liner with DeLane's Deep Shadow and pull in the stamen stems. Shade where they cross and where they come out from the flower with a line of Traditional Raw Umber. Highlight some with a line of Peach Sherbet.

step 30 Form the stamen heads with small Burnt Sienna commas, using the liner. Shade one side of each head with a line of Traditional Raw Umber and highlight with a line of Yellow Ochre. On the three left stamens dot Light Buttermilk on the highlight line.

step 31 Form each leaf with a pointed comma stroke pulled out from the stem. Use the no. 6 round for the large leaves and the no. 4 round for the small leaves. Load with Light Avocado and tip in Midnite Green. Remember to turn the surface to pull the stroke toward you. With the no. 00 liner, pull a vein of DeLane's Deep Shadow up from the stem. Highlight the vein in the lighter part of the leaf with Peach Sherbet.

32] Load the no. 00 liner in Light Avocado. Pull in the lily stem, feathering it into the lily petal with fine lines. Shade the stem where it comes out from under the flower and at its base with Midnite Green. Highlight the stem here and there and where it feathers into the lily with lines of Reindeer Moss Green.

33] Use the no. 00 liner to pull in the tendril with mv. Blue. Shade the tendril with Uniform Blue and highlight it with lv. Blue.
  Paint the stems of the fluffy flowers with Arbor Green in the liner and highlight some with a line of Reindeer Moss Green.
  Use a regular cotton swab to pounce mv. Brown in the heads of the fluffy flowers. In the same manner, stipple Sand very lightly over the entire head. Finish by pouncing Light Buttermilk on one side with the small pointed cotton swab.

34] Apply the spots on just one lily petal at a time. Use a flat brush to dampen the surface with extender. Load the no. 2 round lightly in Traditional Raw Umber, thinned with extra extender. Keep the brush flattened. Note that the spots are long rather than round and are lighter in the light areas of the petals. Start with the spots in the dark areas and work up into the spots in the lighter area without reloading. Go back and reapply the spots that rest in the darker areas of the petals.

35] Repeat the spotting on each petal in the lily.

Bumblebees

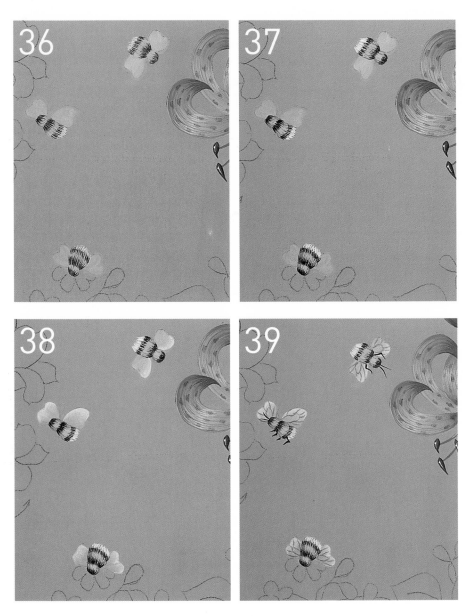

step 36] Work on all the bees at this time. Brush-mix Sand with extender in the no. 4 philbert for transparent color. Brush this on the wings.

Use the no. 00 liner to apply the following colors with fine lines that run lengthwise in each stripe. Pull many lines of Sand in the bee's bottom section. Pull lines of Yellow Ochre in the yellow stripes and Traditional Raw Umber in the dark stripes. Allow the Raw Umber to be transparent.

step 37] Continue to stroke lengthwise lines in the stripes with the following colors. Load the no. 00 liner with a brush mix of Yellow Ochre + Milk Chocolate. Pull lines in the yellow stripes, concentrating more on the sides for shading. In the same way, apply Lamp Black in the dark stripes. Add a few lines of Light Buttermilk in the light bottom section.

step 38] Highlight the middle of the yellow sections with lines of Lemon Yellow. Lightly float Light Buttermilk on one side of the wings.

step 39] Thin Traditional Raw Umber with extender for a transparent load. Detail the cells in the wings. Load the liner with Lamp Black and paint the antennae and legs.

step 40] Load the no. 4 round in Uniform Blue and tip in mv. Blue. Form the middle rear petals with two pressure strokes pulled into the flower's center. Form the rear side petals on the open flowers and open bud with pointed pressure strokes pulled down from their tips.

step 41] Load the no. 6 round in mv. Blue and tip in Uniform Blue. Form the outer throat of the flower with pressure strokes pulled from the flower's center down to the stem.

step 42] Load the no. 00 liner with Payne's Grey. Shade the base of the rear petals with lines pulled out from their base. Shade the top of the throat petals in the same way.
  Load the liner with lv. Blue. Highlight the rear petals with fine lines in an arc shape. Highlight the outer throat with lines pulled up from the stem.

step 43] Load the no. 4 philbert with mv. Blue and tip generously in lv. Blue. Form the foreground petals with a pointed pressure stroke that has a short point and quick fanned pressure. Pull and taper the tail into a fine point as you pull the tail into the flower's center. Rest the tail of each stroke along the edge of the corresponding throat petal.

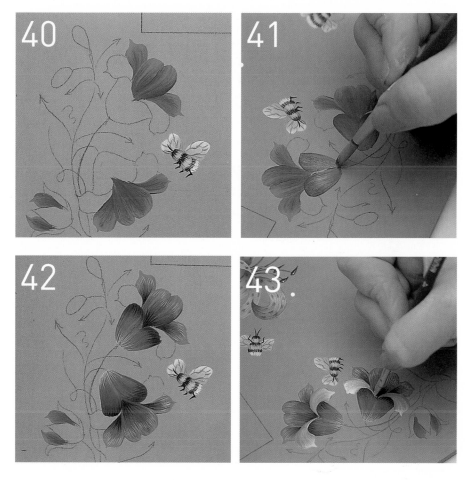

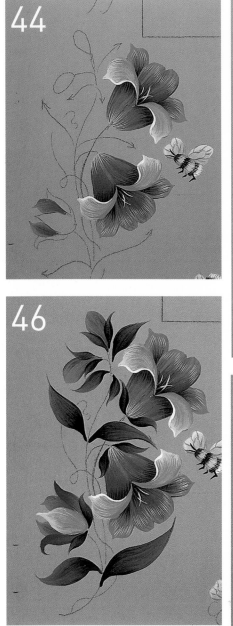

step 44] Use a contour stroke to line the lower edge of the foreground petals with Light Buttermilk on the no. 00 liner brush. Load the liner with Yellow Ochre and pull in the stamens. Shade the base of the stamens with a line of Brandy Wine.

step 45] Load the no. 4 round with mv. Blue and tip in Uniform Blue. Form the side petals on the open bud with pointed comma strokes pulled from the tip to the stem. Load the no. 4 round in mv. Blue and tip in lv. Blue. Form the middle petal on the open bud with a pointed pressure stroke pulled down to the stem.

Load the no. 4 round in Uniform Blue and tip in mv. Blue. Form each closed bud with a fanned comma stroke pulled back to the stem.

step 46] Load the no. 4 round with Arbor Green and tip into Midnite Green. Stroke in the leaves with a pointed comma stroke pulled out from the stem. Load the no. 2 round in the same way. Pull short pointed commas up from the base of all flowers and buds to form the sepals.

step 47] Load the no. 00 liner in mv. Blue and pull veins in all leaves. Load the liner in Arbor Green and pull in all stems. Shade the stems with Midnite Green where they come out from under the flowers or leaves. Highlight with Yellow Ochre.

Use the no. 00 liner to pull in the tendril with DeLane's Deep Shadow. Shade the tendril with a line of Brandy Wine. Highlight with a line of Peach Sherbet.

step 48 Load the no. 4 round in Peach Sherbet and tip in French Mocha. Pull comma strokes from the petals down to the stems to form throats of the individual flowers.

step 49 Form the petals with pressure strokes pulled into the flower's center. Load the no. 4 philbert in Khaki Tan. Tip in Buttermilk for the two petals that overlap the throat. Tip in Sand for the remaining three petals.

step 50 For the unopened buds, pull tapered pressure and comma strokes back to the stem. For the light flowers, load the no. 4 philbert in Khaki Tan and tip in Sand. For the peach buds, load in French Mocha and tip in Peach Sherbet.

step 51 Highlight the base of the throat petal with fine lines of Sand pulled up from the stem. Brush-mix French Mocha + Rookwood Red in the no. 00 liner and pull shading lines down from between petals at the top of the throat.

step 52 Load the no. 00 liner in French Mocha. Pull fine lines out from the U-shaped opening on the three rear petals in each flower. Line the crest of the opening with Rookwood Red. Use the stylus to dot Yellow Ochre in the opening of each flower.

step 53] Paint the leaves, using the no. 6 round for the large leaves and the no. 4 round for the small ones. Load in Arbor Green and tip in Midnite Green. Form each leaf with two pointed comma strokes pulled out from the stem to the tip. Keep the strokes flat along the vein of the leaf and fan the bristles on the outer edges of the leaf.

step 54] Load the no. 4 round with Arbor Green and tip in Reindeer Moss Green. To form the turned edges, pull pointed commas toward the stem. Pull a long point and apply quick pressure, leaning into the leaf. As you release pressure, take the tail of the stroke along the edge of the leaf.

step 55] Load the no. 2 round in Arbor Green and tip in Midnite Green. Form the sepals on the flowers and buds with pointed comma strokes pulled out from the stem. Load the no. 00 liner with Arbor Green and pull in all stems. Brush-mix Arbor Green + Midnite Green and, with a line, shade the stems where they come out from under another object. Highlight with a line of Reindeer Moss Green.

step 56] Load the no. 00 liner in mv. Blue and pull a vein in each leaf. Also pull in the tendrils with mv. Blue. Shade the tendrils with Uniform Blue and highlight with lv. Blue.

step 57 | Load the no. 6 round in Khaki Tan and tip in Sand. Form the outer petals with pointed comma strokes pulled from the tip back to the bowl. The large lower petal will take two strokes that are flat on the inside edge and fanned open on the other.

step 58 | Form the inside of the bowl with a fan stroke pulled down into the opening. Load the no. 6 round in Rookwood Red and tip in Gooseberry Pink. Set the brush down on the dotted line with the ferrule resting on the surface. The brush tip is inside the bowl. Fan the brush open until it hits the sides of the opening. Push the brush to the outer edge, then pull it down into the bowl.

step 59 | With the no. 10 flat, float mv. Violet shading at the base of the side petals. Walk the color out into the body of the petal and soften the faint edge with the dry mop brush. In the large lower petal apply angular floats to indicate puckers in the petal.

step 60 | Deepen the shading on the four side petals with a light float of Rookwood Red. Also shade the base of the fan stroke with a float of Rookwood Red. Slide on the chisel to coax streaks up into the petal while the surface and float remain wet.

step 61 | Use the no. 10 flat to tint one side of three side petals with a float of Gooseberry Pink. Soften the faint edge of the float with the mop. Float a highlight with Buttermilk along the top edge of the two lower side petals with the no. 10 flat. In the same manner, highlight the light sides of the middle petal.

step 62 | Load the no. 5 toler generously with Flesh Tone and apply a thick line of heavy paint to form the wavy opening of the bowl.

step 63 Immediately load and flatten the no. 4 round with mv. Red. Beginning with the stroke in the middle of the bowl, set the brush in the middle of the thick paint line and pull down to the base of the bowl. Reload, flatten the round again and, in the same way, pull a curved stroke beside the first. At the end of this stroke, slide the chisel along the base of the first stroke to shape the lower edge of the bowl.

step 64 Continue to pull strokes down from the wet Flesh Tone to complete the bowl. Load the no. 00 liner in Flesh Tone and line the rim of the fan stroke with a broken line.

step 65 Load the liner in Buttermilk and line the opening where it turns from front to back. Stipple pollen at the base of the opening with the liner. Begin with a brush mix of Rookwood Red + Midnite Green and stipple a soft circular shape. Over this shape, stipple Arbor Green and then highlight toward the top with dots of Yellow Ochre.

step 66 Load the no. 9 toler in Arbor Green and tip in Midnite Green. Form the long leaves with a pointed comma pulled out from the stem.

step 67 Load the no. 4 round with Arbor Green and tip in Reindeer Moss Green for the pointed commas that form the turned edges. Pull a long point down from the top, apply quick pressure into the leaf and then slide the tail along the edge of the leaf.

step 68 Load the no. 00 liner with Gooseberry Pink and pull a broken center vein up into both leaves. Load the liner in Arbor Green and pull in the stem. With lines of Midnite Green, shade the stem where a tendril or leaf will cross. Highlight the stem with a line of Reindeer Moss Green.

Vetch

step 69 Load the no. 4 round with DeLane's Deep Shadow and tip in Peach Sherbet. To form the side petals, pull comma strokes down to the stem. Load the no. 4 round in DeLane's Deep Shadow and tip in Yellow Ochre. Stroke in each center petal with a comma pulled down to the stem.

step 70 Load the no. 2 round in Midnite Green. Pull pointed comma strokes out from the stem to form the sepals. Keep them from touching each other. Load the no. 00 liner with Sable Brown and form the stamens with hatpin strokes pulled out from the flower.

step 71 Load the no. 4 round in Midnite Green and tip in Light Avocado for the leaves. Pull a comma stroke down to the stem on one side of the leaf. Reload and pull a pointed comma down from the tip. Reload and pull a comma on the remaining side of the leaf. Complete one leaf before moving to the next so the wet strokes will blend together along the sides.

step 72 Use the no. 00 liner to pull a center vein in each leaf with French Grey Blue. Paint the stems with Light Avocado. Shade the stems with a brush mix of Light Avocado + Midnite Green. Highlight with a line of Reindeer Moss Green.

Butterfly

step 73 For the wings, load the no. 2 round in mv. Blue and tip in lv. Blue. Pull two fan strokes back to the body for the top wing, and one fan stroke for the lower wing.

step 74 Load the no. 00 liner in Traditional Raw Umber and pull a slender comma for the body. Pull two antennae out from the head. Transfer the pattern for the cell structure or apply freehand. Load the liner with thinned Light Buttermilk and paint the delicate lines.

Lettering and Finishing

step 75 Apply tape on both sides of the narrow straight stripes and burnish the edges with the Bondo spreader. Apply Arbor Green in the space between the tape with the no. 00 liner. Use the liner loaded in Arbor Green to stroke in the curved lines at the top.

Remove the tape. Dot Arbor Green in the corners with the stylus tool.

Load the no. 00 liner in Honey Brown and fill in the lettering.

step 76 Shade the lower strokes in the lettering with lines of Brandy Wine.

step 77 Highlight the upper strokes in the lettering with a line of Yellow Ochre.

Erase any visible transfer lines and apply several coats of DecoArt Dura-Clear Satin Varnish with the 2-inch (51mm) flat. When the varnish is thoroughly dry, assemble the album.

Completed Memory Album

Clock with Columbines

The first time I saw columbines, I was walking in the hills of a southern Wisconsin park reserve. The beautiful colors and unusual petal formation captivated my attention, and I soon became a fan. Later I discovered that columbines had also been cultivated in dwarf and larger sizes for the home garden, with some even having double ruffled petals. Although they appear to be delicate and fragile, they are surprisingly hardy plants, and varieties of columbines can be found around the world. They usually are bicolored, and often the same plant will produce a variety of colors. I never tire of painting columbines, and each time I do, my mind wanders back to that walk in the park so many years ago.

SURFACE

Wooden clock back, available from Painters Paradise
(See Resources on page 126.)

MAUREEN MCNAUGHTON BRUSHES

no. 4 round, no. 6 round, no. 8 round, no. 5 toler, no. 00 liner,
no. 0 mop, no. 10 flat, no. 12 flat, 2-inch (51mm) flat

ADDITIONAL SUPPLIES

extender: water + DecoArt Easy Float (3:1); gold leaf adhesive;
old flat brush (for applying gold adhesive); gold leaf; velvet cloth; light transfer paper;
DecoArt DuraClear Satin Varnish; Roman Numerals, ⅝-inch (16mm) plastic
self-adhesive numbers, available from Walnut Hollow, item 554 (See Resources on
page 126); clock quartz movement for ⅜-inch (10mm) thick surface, available from
Walnut Hollow (See Resources on page 126.)

Palette

DecoArt Americana Acrylic Paints *indicates colors that DO NOT require extender

Antique Teal +
Charcoal Grey
(2:1)
(background)

Jade Green

Green Mist

Avocado

*Deep Teal

*Plantation
Pine

Baby Blue

Country Blue

*Deep
Midnight Blue

Violet Haze

*dv. Violet:
Royal Purple +
Payne's Grey
(2:1)

Baby Pink

Spice Pink

Gooseberry
Pink

*mv. Red
Violet: Antique
Mauve +
Cranberry
Wine (2:1)

*Cranberry
Wine

French Vanilla

Yellow Ochre

Desert Sand

Khaki Tan

Mississippi
Mud

This pattern may be hand-traced or photocopied for personal use only. Enlarge at 150 percent to bring up to full size.

Do not be constricted by the pattern. It is a guideline only as to the length and width of the strokes.

The letters "w" and "c" stand for warm and cool.

Surface Preparation, Warm Leaves & Cool Leaves

Surface Preparation

step 1 Prepare the surface as instructed on pages 10-11. Basecoat all surfaces of the clock with Antique Teal + Charcoal Grey (2:1). Save some color for touch-ups. When the surface is dry, trace on the pattern with light transfer paper. If using the plastic self-adhesive numbers, just put a mark where each number will go.

Warm Leaves

step 2 Use the no. 4 round for small strokes and the no. 6 round for larger strokes. Load in Avocado and tip in Jade Green. If right-handed, do the left-side stroke, then the middle stroke and finish with the right-side stroke. Reverse if left-handed. Each stroke is a pointed comma with a short point and quick pressure, pulled back to the stem. Fan the brush open when required for width.

step 3 Load the no. 00 liner in Cranberry Wine and pull a center vein out from the stem in each leaf. Remember to always turn your surface so you can clearly see the path of the brushstroke as it is pulled.

step 4 With the no. 10 or no. 12 flat, float Plantation Pine on some dark edges. To keep this dark color from getting in the light areas, pull the color down toward the stem where possible. Mop it off the light tips if required.

Cool Leaves

step 5 Use the no. 4 round for small strokes and the no. 6 round for larger strokes. Load in Deep Teal and tip in Green Mist.

step 6 Load the no. 00 liner in Cranberry Wine and pull a center vein out from the stem in each leaf.

step 7 With the no. 10 or no. 12 flat, float Country Blue as a highlight on some light edges on the cool leaves.

step 8] Load the no. 4 round in Khaki Tan and tip in Mississippi Mud. Form the four rear jester petals with a pointed comma stroke pulled out from the flower, beginning with the rear petals. Do not do the center petal at this time.

Load the no. 8 round in mv. Red Violet and tip in Gooseberry Pink. Gooseberry Pink is very opaque, so don't dip in too deeply. Form the five leaf-shaped petals with a pointed pressure stroke pulled back into the flower. Pull a point and then lay the brush down to the ferrule. Fan the brush open to achieve the desired width, if required. Retrace the outline of the round petals on top of the leaf petals when the color is dry.

step 9] Load the no. 5 toler in Khaki Tan and tip in Mississippi Mud. Form the small knob at the end of each painted jester petal with a small teardrop stroke pulled out from the point of the petal.

Load the no. 6 round in Mississippi Mud and tip in Desert Sand. Form the four round petals with pressure strokes pulled into the unpainted foreground petal. You may need to fan the brush open to achieve the desired width.

Load the no. 00 liner in Gooseberry Pink. Fix the tips of the leaf petals into better points.

step 10] Use the no. 12 flat to float dv. Violet shading on the round petals, next to the unpainted foreground petal. Coax out some streaks by sliding on the chisel.

Float dv. Violet at the base of the jester petals. Also float it at the base of the leaf petals, between the round petals and next to the foreground petal. Mop as required to soften the color.

Mix mv. Red Violet with a touch of Gooseberry Pink. Float a sliver of highlight on the edge of the two leaf petals where they overlap the neighboring jester petal.

Petal Names

Jester petals are long and slender with a knob at the end, similar to the points on a jester's hat.

Leaf petals are red with a blunt point on the tip.

Round petals are the same color as the jester petals because the two are actually parts of one petal. Refer to the foreground petal in each flower.

step 11 Load the no. 5 toler in Gooseberry Pink and tip in French Vanilla. Form the turned edges on the outside edge of the outer round petals with a pointed comma stroke as follows: Pull a long line, starting on the outer edge of the petal. Apply quick pressure, leaning into the petal. Taper and pull the tail down along the outer edge of the petal.

Use the no. 00 liner to extend the light tip of the turned edges a little farther with a line of French Vanilla.

Load the no. 6 round in Khaki Tan and tip in French Vanilla. Pull in the foreground petal with a comma stroke with a long curved tail.

Load the no. 5 toler in Khaki Tan and form the knob at the end of the petal with a teardrop stroke.

step 12 With the no. 12 flat, create a turned edge on the foreground petal by shading under it with a float of Gooseberry Pink. (See the single petal standing alone off to the side.) Then float Mississippi Mud shading on the turned edges of the outer round petals, next to the foreground petal.

With the no. 10 flat, deepen the shading in the valleys of the turned edge on the foreground petal with a sheer float of Mississippi Mud.

Use French Vanilla on a no. 00 liner to line the turned edge on the foreground petal. Extend slightly down the sides. On the tips of the jester petals, line one side of the knob with French Vanilla and cross the line over to extend along the other side of the petal.

step 13 Over a damp surface, use a no. 12 flat to float Yellow Ochre along one side of the top three leaf petals.

With a no. 10 flat, float a sliver of Yellow Ochre along the upper edge of the slender part of the foreground petal.

Still using the no. 10 flat, float Violet Haze on the right side of the remaining leaf petals, in the darker area.

step 14 Load the no. 4 round in Violet Haze and tip in Deep Midnight Blue. Beginning with the two rear petals, form the four jester petals with a pointed comma stroke pulled out from the flower. Do not do the center petal at this time.

Load the no. 6 round in Deep Midnight Blue and tip in Violet Haze. Form the three round petals with pressure strokes pulled into the unpainted foreground petals. You may need to fan the brush open to achieve the desired width.

step 15 Load the no. 5 toler in Violet Haze and tip in Deep Midnight Blue. Form the small knob at the end of each petal with a small teardrop stroke pulled out from the point of the petal.

With a no. 12 flat, float Deep Midnight Blue shading at the base of the round petals and the jester petals if required. Coax out streaks by sliding on the chisel. Deepen the base of the above shading with a float of dv. Violet on a no. 10 flat.

step 16 Load the no. 6 round in mv. Red Violet and tip in Spice Pink. Form the three leaf-shaped petals with a pointed pressure stroke pulled down from the tip. Pull a point and then lay the brush down to the ferrule. Fan the brush open if required for width. Wiggle the stroke for shape variety as you pull back into the unpainted foreground petal.

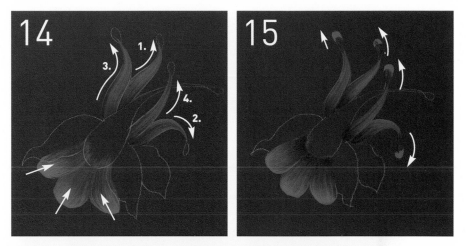

step 17 Float shading at the base of the leaf petals with dv. Violet on a no. 12 flat.

Load the no. 6 round in Violet Haze and tip in Baby Blue. Form the foreground petal with a long comma stroke.

Load the no. 5 toler in Violet Haze. Form the knob at the end of this petal with a teardrop stroke pulled out from the point.

step 18 Create a turned edge on the foreground petal by shading under it with a float of Deep Midnight Blue on a no. 10 flat.

Line the turned edge on the foreground petal with Baby Blue on a no. 00 liner. Extend slightly down the sides.

On the tips of the jester petals, line one side of the knob with Baby Blue and cross the line over to extend along the other side of the petal. Again, use the no. 00 liner.

With a mix of mv. Red Violet and a touch of Spice Pink, use the no. 10 flat to float a sliver of a highlight on the edge of the leaf petals where they overlap each other and where they overlap the jester petals.

step 19 Use a no. 10 flat for all the floated colors in this step. First float a sliver of Baby Blue on the jester petal second from the right, on the lower edge of the foreground petal, and along the tip of the middle round petal.

Next float a sliver of Baby Pink on the left edge of the left jester petal and on the top edge of the slender part of the foreground petal.

Float Yellow Ochre on the upper light edge of the two right leaf petals.

Float Violet Haze on the upper edge of the left leaf petal.

Use the no. 00 liner to pull in five stamen stems with a brush mix of Avocado + Jade Green. With the same color on the liner tip, stipple in a mushroom-shaped cluster at the end of the stems (see the top stamen illustration to the right of the columbine).

Stipple Plantation Pine in the heads and line some of the stamen stems, as you see in the middle stamen illustration.

Stipple Yellow Ochre in the heads, as you see in the bottom stamen illustration. Add stamens to the pink and yellow columbine as well.

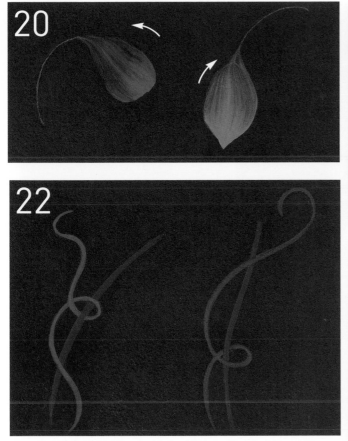

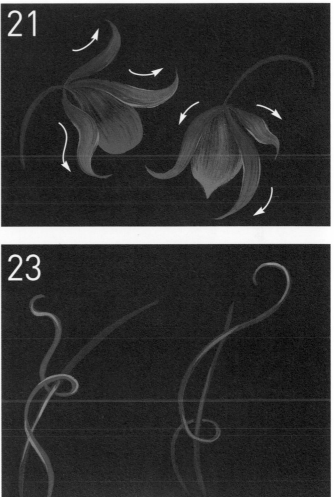

Buds

step 20] Form the buds with pointed comma and comma strokes pulled down to the stem. For the violet buds load the no. 6 round in dv. Violet and tip in Violet Haze. For the pink buds load the no. 6 round in mv. Red Violet and tip in Gooseberry Pink.

step 21] Load the no. 5 toler in Jade Green and tip in Avocado. Form the sepals with pointed comma strokes pulled out from the stem. Wiggle the stroke or pull longer tails for shape variety.
Pull in all stems with Avocado on a no. 00 liner.

Tendrils

step 22] Pull in the blue tendril on the upper left of the design with a brush mix of Violet Haze + Deep Midnight Blue on a no. 00 liner.
Pull in the lower red tendril with mv. Red Violet.

Stems

step 23] Use the no. 00 liner to highlight some stems with a long line of Jade Green. For placement, look for the crest of the curved stems.
On some stems, add a sparkle in the middle of the highlight with a shorter highlight line of Yellow Ochre.
Highlight the blue tendril with a line of Baby Blue.
Highlight the red tendril with a line of Gooseberry Pink.
Then add a sparkle to the top highlight on the red tendril with a shorter line of Yellow Ochre.

Clock Face Border, Gold Leafing & Finishing

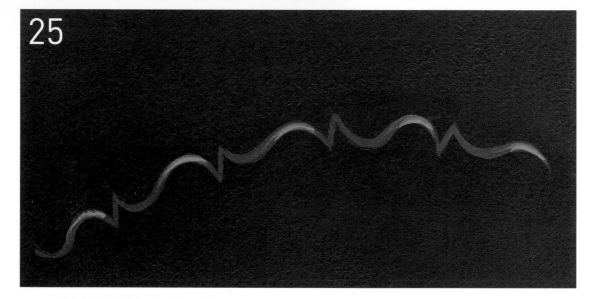

Clock Face Border

step 24] Mix mv. Red Violet + Mississippi Mud (2:1). Load the no. 00 liner and pull in the border with S shapes, which straddle the line and go from one notch to the next.

step 25] Then connect the S shapes with a straight line. Highlight each S shape with a line of Gooseberry Pink.

Gold Leafing

step 26] When the painting is complete, apply gold leafing on the routed edge along the outer rim of the clock and the heart cutout at the top, as instructed on page 66.

Finishing

step 27] Erase any visible transfer lines. Protect the front and back surfaces of the clock with several coats of DecoArt DuraClear Satin Varnish applied with the 2-inch (51mm) flat brush.

step 28] Allow the varnish to dry for several days. Then attach the plastic self-adhesive numbers.

step 29] Attach clockworks and hands according to package directions.

Completed Columbine Clock

Floral Tray
with Scrollwork

This beautiful bentwood tray was designed and made by my good friends Jacques Bérubé and Manon Larose. Its curved lines inspired an elegant design with flowers that I think would have been found in a Victorian garden.

The monochromatic scrolls provide the perfect frame. They are painted with dark and light tones of the background hue, so they do not compete for attention with the colorful flowers.

Each petal and leaf is formed with brushstrokes. When the flower shape is formed, it is enhanced with extra detail to bring the flower to life.

SURFACE

Victorian Tray, item 59, available from La Maison BeL'art
(See Resources on page 126.)

MAUREEN MCNAUGHTON BRUSHES

no. 00 liner, no. 2 liner, no. 2 round, no. 4 round, no. 6 round, no. 8 round, no. 6 philbert,
no. 1 mop, no. 6 flat, no. 12 flat, 1-inch (25mm) basecoat/varnish brush

MCNAUGHTON 200 SERIES PROFESSIONAL BRUSHES

no. 6 round, no. 10 round

ADDITIONAL SUPPLIES

extender: water + DecoArt Easy Float (3:1), stylus, Krylon 18K Gold Leafing Pen,
gold leaf adhesive, old flat brush (for applying gold leaf adhesive),
gold leaf, velvet cloth, light transfer paper,
DecoArt DuraClear Satin Varnish

Palette

DecoArt Americana Acrylic Paints *indicates colors that DO NOT require extender*

Driftwood +
Dusty Rose (1:1)
(background)
Save some for
touch-ups.

Light
Buttermilk

Buttermilk

mv. Ivory:
Buttermilk +
Antique White
(1:1)

Antique White

Khaki Tan

Pineapple

Moon Yellow

Camel

Marigold

*Honey Brown

*Milk
Chocolate

Mississippi
Mud

Reindeer Moss
Green

mv. Green:
Celery Green +
Charcoal Grey
(8:1)

mv. Warm
Green:
Avocado +
Mauve
(8:1)

dv. Green:
Black Green +
Avocado
(2:1)

Mint Julep
Green

mv. Cool
Green: Arbor
Green +
Antique Rose
(6:1)

Winter Blue

Light French
Blue

French Grey
Blue

*Soft Peach

French Mocha
(inside tray)

mv. Red:
French Mocha
+ Traditional
Burnt Umber
(1:1)

*Antique
Maroon
(outside
edges)

Lilac

Plum

Royal Purple

Mauve

*Cranberry
Wine

*Black Plum

Toffee

Cashmere
Beige

Mink Tan

mv. Brown:
Khaki Tan +
Mississippi
Mud
(1:1)

This pattern may be hand-traced or photocopied for personal use only.
Enlarge at 210 percent to bring up to full size.

Surface Preparation and Leaves

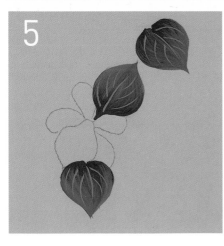

Surface Preparation

1. Prepare the surface as instructed on pages 10-11.

2. Basecoat the inside floor of the tray with a mix of Driftwood + Dusty Rose (1:1). Save some color for touch-ups. Basecoat the inside walls of the tray with French Mocha. Basecoat the outside surfaces and feet of the tray Antique Maroon.

3. When the surface is dry, trace on the pattern with light transfer paper.

Iris Leaves

step 1. Load the no. 6 round in mv. Green and tip in dv. Green. Form each leaf with two pointed comma strokes pulled from the stem to the leaf tip. These strokes may have a wiggle along the sides. Take the strokes right over the hydrangea flower.

step 2. Load the no. 4 round in mv. Green and tip in Reindeer Moss Green. Form the turned edge on the right leaf with two pointed comma strokes pulled down from the tip of the leaf. Form the turned edge on the left leaf with just one pointed comma stroke pulled down from the tip of the leaf. Use the no. 00 liner to pull in a center vein in each leaf with French Grey Blue.

step 3. Use the liner to extend the darker end of the turned edge with mv. Green. In the same manner, extend the light tip of the turned edge with Pineapple. Also line the valley between the two strokes that form the turned edge on the right leaf. Darken the vein at the base of the leaf in the darker area with a line of Plum.

Violet Leaves

step 4. Load the no. 4 round in mv. Warm Green and tip in dv. Green. Complete each leaf with two strokes that finish with a point at the leaf tip. On those leaves that rest under the violets, start the strokes on top of the flower.

step 5. Load the no. 00 liner in a brush mix of French Grey Blue + Light French Blue. Pull in a center vein and disconnected side veins in each violet leaf.

Hydrangea Leaves

step 6] Form these leaves with pointed comma strokes pulled out from the stem. Load the no. 6 round in mv. Warm Green and tip cautiously in Black Plum.

step 7] Brush-mix Honey Brown with a touch of Camel in the no. 00 liner. Form a highlight arc in each section with many fine lines. Make the highlight on one half of each leaf a little lighter with additional fine lines of Camel.

Brush-mix Plum + Lilac in the liner and pull a center vein in each leaf.

Calla Lilly Leaves

step 8] Use the no. 8 round for the two large leaves behind the flowers and the no. 6 round for the smaller leaf below. Load in mv. Cool Green and tip in dv. Green. Form each leaf with two pointed comma strokes pulled from the stem out to the leaf tip. Go right over the lilies.

Form the turned edges on two of the leaves with pointed comma strokes pulled back toward the stem. Load the no. 4 round in mv. Cool Green and tip in Mint Julep Green. Pull a long line, then apply quick pressure, leaning into the leaf. Pull and release pressure while bringing the tail back over to the side of the leaf.

step 9] Extend both ends of the turned edge into better points with the no. 00 liner. Use Mint Julep Green at the light end and mv. Cool Green at the dark end. On the lower leaf, extend the turned edge to form a broad stem with mv. Cool Green.

Load the liner in Pineapple and accent the valley of the turned edge with a thin line.

Use the liner to pull in a center vein with mv. Green.

Pull a few Reindeer Moss Green highlight lines in the stem of the lower leaf.

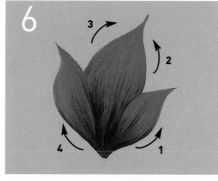

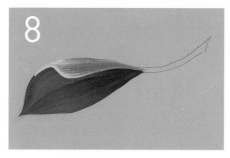

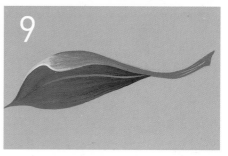

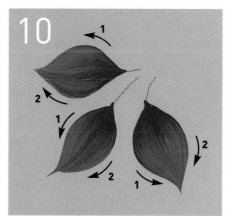

Small Leaves on Left

step 10] Load the no. 4 round in mv. Cool Green and tip in dv. Green. Form each leaf with two pointed comma strokes pulled from the stem to the leaf tip.

step 11] Load the no. 00 liner in mv. Green. Pull in the leaf stem and center vein with a curved line. Then highlight where the line enters the leaf with a shorter line of Reindeer Moss Green.

step 12 Retrace the flower pattern over the dry leaves. Basecoat the flowers that overlap the leaves with the background color.

step 13 Load the no. 6 round in Antique White and tip cautiously in French Grey Blue. Form the top middle petal with two tapered pressure strokes pulled down from the petal tip to the flower center. Go right over the other petals.

Load the no. 8 round in Antique White and tip in Royal Purple. Form the lower middle petal with a fan stroke pulled back to the flower center.

step 14 **Top Petals:** Load the no. 8 round in Antique White and tip in Plum. Form the top right petal with a curved fan stroke that finishes with a point at the flower center.

Load the no. 6 round in Antique White and tip in Plum. Form the top left petal with two comma strokes that finish at the flower center.

Lower petals: Load the no. 6 round loaded in Antique White and tip in Plum. Form the right petal with two comma strokes pulled back to the flower center. Form the left petal with two pointed comma strokes pulled from the outer petal tip back to the center. Wiggle the outer edge of each stroke to form the waves in the petal.

step 15 Use the no. 00 liner to pull lines of Camel up from the base of the top two purple petals.

Form the turned edges with one or two pointed comma strokes pulled back into the flower. The strokes start and finish on the edge of the petal.

For the lower side petals and the upper blue petal, load the no. 4 round in Plum and tip in Winter Blue. Extend the light tip a little further with the no. 00 liner. Line the valley in the turn with Lilac.

For the remaining two turned edges load the no. 4 round in Plum and tip in Lilac. Extend the light tip a little further with the no. 00 liner.

With a no. 12 flat, float Royal Purple on the upper right edge of the lower fan stroke petal and also on the upper left edge of the upper fan stroke petal.

step 16 Use a no. 12 flat to reflect the blue from the hydrangeas on the outer edge of the lower fan stroke petal and the lower side petal on the left with floated tints of French Grey Blue. Dampen the surface first. Apply the color and mop it up into the petal.

With the no. 12 flat, float Plum under the turned edge on the upper left petal and extend it under the area where the beard will sit.

Lighten the right tip of the lower middle petal with a float of Winter Blue over a damp surface.

Directions for painting the beard are in the next step. Use this illustration as a guide for placement.

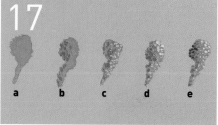

Iris Beard

step 17 **a.** Load the no. 4 round with Honey Brown and stipple in the entire shape of the beard.

b. Load the no. 00 liner in Milk Chocolate. Stipple shading on the underside of the beards and allow a few stipples in the middle area.

c. Load the no. 00 liner in Camel. Stipple dots on the other side and allow some to drift toward the middle.

d. Load the no. 00 liner in Moon Yellow. Stipple highlight dots in the light area.

e. Load the no. 00 liner in Cranberry Wine. Stipple a few dots on the dark side of the beards.

Calla Lily

step 18 Load the no. 6 round in Khaki Tan and tip in Buttermilk. Form the rear petals with fanned pressure strokes pulled down into the turned edges of the foreground petals. The dotted lines on the pattern indicate the direction in which to pull the strokes.

Load the no. 6 round in Buttermilk and tip in Khaki Tan. Form the outer throat petal with strokes pulled down from the unpainted turned edges to the stem. On the left lily, do the right petal first.

step 19 Load the no. 00 liner in Buttermilk. On the rear petals, line the V-shaped notches between the strokes into U shapes and pull fine lines down into the petal so the entire outer edge is light.

Trace on the pattern for the turned edges. Float mv. Green out from the base of the rear petal with the no. 12 flat. Float mv. Green in the valleys under the turned edges.

Intensify the base of some green shading with a smaller float of dv. Green.

step 20 Load the no. 4 round in mv. Ivory and tip in Light Buttermilk. Form the turned edges with pointed comma strokes pulled back toward the stem. The turn on the right lily is formed with two strokes. Extend the light tips into finer points with the no. 00 liner.

Pull in the flower stem with mv. Green and pull lines up into the base of the flower with the liner.

To add the pistils, use the lily on the right for placement and the lettered steps in the middle for painting instructions.

a. Use the liner to fill in the lily pistils with Honey Brown.

b. With the liner, stipple Milk Chocolate on the right side of the pistils. Let some stipples drift toward the middle area.

c. Still using the no. 00 liner, stipple Camel on the left side, drifting some stipples toward the middle.

d. Stipple a few additional highlights on the light area with Moon Yellow.

[step 21] Load the no. 4 round in Royal Purple and tip in Lilac. Form the top and side petals that lay over leaves (marked "a") with tapered pressure strokes pulled into the center of the flower.

Load the no. 4 round in Lilac and tip in Royal Purple. Form the top petals that lay on the background (marked "b") with tapered pressure strokes pulled into the center of the flower.

Load the no. 4 round in Winter Blue and tip in Royal Purple. Pull in the remaining side petal (marked "c") resting on the pink background with tapered pressure strokes pulled into the center of the flower.

Load the no. 4 round in Lilac and tip in Plum. Form the large lower petal on all violets with two pointed pressure strokes pulled back to the center. Fan the stroke on the outer edges of the petal and keep the inside edge straight.

With the no. 00 liner loaded in Lilac, pull lines out from the center of the flower on this petal.

[step 22] Detail the large lower petal with the no. 00 liner as follows:

a. Pull lines of Moon Yellow out from the center.

b. Pull shorter lines of Honey Brown out from the center.

c. Place a small dab of mv. Green at the top of the petal to form the opening.

d. Stroke dv. Green as shading on the top edge of this green dab.

e. Frame the opening with small contour strokes of Light Buttermilk with the liner.

[step 23] Still using the no. 00 liner, pull in the stems to the violets and the curl to the left with mv. Green. Highlight some stems with lines of Reindeer Moss Green.

Hydrangea

step 24 Stipple the following colors in the mushroom-shaped flower head with the no. 10 Professional Round. Do not wash out the brush between colors. Just scrub out the excess on a dry paper towel. Residual color helps to tone down the next color.

Stipple Light French Blue over the entire head. This is opaque coverage with fuzzy edges. Brush-mix Light French Blue + French Grey Blue. Stipple this color lightly over the entire flower head. Brush-mix Plum + French Grey Blue. Stipple this color on the lower third of the head. Stipple Winter Blue on the upper third.

step 25 The hydrangea is a dense cluster of many small florets whose stems all attach to the main stem. A full floret has four petals; however, in most flowers you may only see one, two or three of these petals. Be certain to leave spaces between the petals, as the blue stippling underneath suggests depth.

Form the petals for the individual florets with pressure strokes that finish with feathery ends. Pull the strokes toward the floret's center, but leave an opening in the middle. Pull darker petals throughout the head with the no. 6 philbert loaded with a brush mix of Winter Blue + Light Buttermilk. Pull medium-value petals throughout the flower head with the no. 6 philbert loaded with Buttermilk. Load the no. 6 philbert in Light Buttermilk. Form florets in the upper third of the flower head and allow some to fall in the middle area.

step 26 Stipple Mauve in the center of each floret with the no. 6 Professional round brush.

To apply a transparent glaze of Cranberry Wine in the lower third of the flower head, first use the no. 12 flat to dampen the entire head with extender. Then load the no. 6 philbert lightly with a brush mix of Cranberry Wine + extender. Immediately brush this transparent color in the shaded area of the flower head. Immediately diffuse the color by brushing over it very lightly with the no. 1 mop.

Using the stylus tool, place small dots over the pink stippling in the middle of each floret. Dot Marigold in the darker florets and in some of the middle-value florets. Dot Moon Yellow in the middle-value florets, and also in some dark and some light florets nearby. Dot Pineapple in the light florets and some middle-value ones nearby.

Pull in the stems with the no. 00 liner loaded in Mississippi Mud. Highlight some stems with a line of Reindeer Moss Green.

Bell Flower

step 27] Load the no. 4 round in mv. Green and tip in Antique White. Pull in the side petals with pointed comma strokes pulled back to the stem. Pull in the petal closest to the hydrangea first. Without reloading, pull in the other side petal. It will be darker because the tipping color is partially depleted.

Load the no. 4 round in Khaki Tan and tip in Buttermilk. Form the center petal with two pointed pressure strokes pulled from the petal tip back to the stem. Do the stroke closest to the hydrangea first. Without reloading, do the other stroke.

step 28] In the no. 00 liner, brush-mix mv. Green + Plum. Pull many fine shading lines out from the base of those side petals positioned on the side of the flower farthest away from the hydrangeas. With the same color pull in the stamen stems with lines.

Load the liner with Buttermilk. Accent the tip of the lighter side petal with a small comma stroke pulled back toward the center petal. Do the same on the dark side petal with mv. Ivory.

With a small stylus tool, dot in the pollen at the ends of the stamen stems with Camel. Then place a few dots of Moon Yellow toward the light side of the flower.

Load the no. 00 liner with mv. Green and pull in their delicate stems with fine lines. In the liner, brush-mix mv. Green + dv. Green. Shade the stem where it comes out from under leaves, stems or the hydrangeas with a line. Highlight some stems with a line of Reindeer Moss Green.

Fuzzy Weed

step 29] **a.** Load the no. 6 flat in mv. Green and scoop up a small blob of Lilac on the corner. Do not blend. Stipple or touch the chisel to the palette and you should see a green line with a lilac blob at the end.

b. Starting at the top of the weed

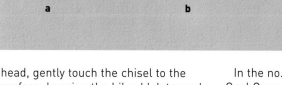

head, gently touch the chisel to the surface, keeping the Lilac blob toward the weed top.

c. Keep touching, staggering these flat brush stipples, until the entire head is completed. Reload as required. The stipples will become fainter as the corner load becomes depleted. Strive to have some strongly colored stipples in the middle of the flower head. Load the no. 00 liner with mv. Green and pull in stems.

Stems and Tendrils

step 30] Pull in the iris stems with the no. 2 liner loaded in mv. Cool Green. This stem is the thicker one that carries through the design and out the right side behind the calla lily leaf.

In the no. 00 liner, brush-mix mv. Cool Green + dv. Green. Shade the stem where it comes out from under leaves and flowers with fine lines.

Highlight with lines of Reindeer Moss Green.

step 31] To make calla lily stems, load the no. 2 liner with mv. Green and pull in any part of the stem remaining on each flower. Don't forget the piece of stem coming out from beneath the lower leaf.

In the no. 00 liner, brush-mix mv. Green + dv. Green. Shade the stem where it comes out from under the leaves with fine lines.

step 32] Pull in the tendrils with the no. 00 liner loaded in French Grey Blue. Highlight where the tendril crosses over a stem or itself with a line of Winter Blue.

Scrolls

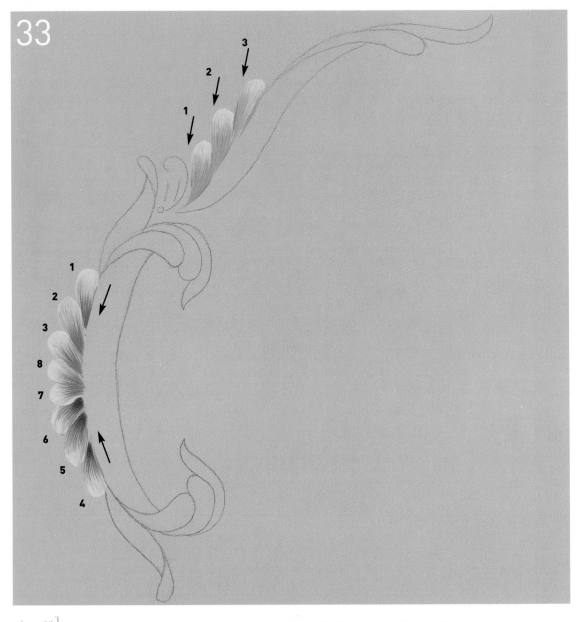

step 33 Note that numbers on the pattern (page 107) indicate different types of strokes, while numbers on the scroll illustration (above) indicate the order of the strokes.

For strokes marked "1" on the pattern, load the no. 4 round in French Mocha and tip in Toffee. Pull these pressure strokes into the unpainted C-shaped scroll and the long S-shaped scroll. Along the C shape, start with the outer strokes and work back toward the middle shape.

Load the no. 00 liner in mv. Red. Pull lines up from the base of each stroke (shown on some strokes along the C-shaped scroll).

Follow with shorter lines of Antique Maroon (shown on some strokes along the C-shaped scroll).

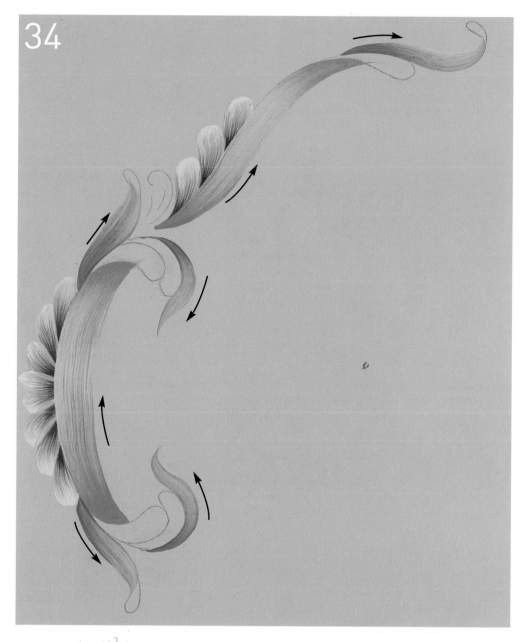

34

step 34 For strokes marked "2" on the pattern, use the no. 8 round for the C-shaped scroll and the no. 6 round for the S-shaped scroll.

Load in Cashmere Beige and tip in mv. Brown. Pull in the C-shaped and the S-shaped scrolls with long pointed comma strokes.

Float mv. Brown at the light end of these strokes with the no. 12 flat.

Load the no. 2 liner in Cashmere Beige. Pull lines through the middle area of both scrolls to lighten the area.

For strokes marked "3" on the pattern, use the no. 4 round for small strokes and the no. 6 round for larger ones. Load in Cashmere Beige and tip in mv. Red. Pull in these shapes with pointed comma strokes.

Scrolls, continued

step 35] Load the no. 2 round in Toffee. Pull in the smaller comma stroke seen at the outer tip of the strokes marked "3" on the pattern.

For strokes marked "4" on the pattern, load the no. 4 round in French Mocha and tip in Toffee. Pull in the comma stroke that forms this shape.

For strokes marked "5" on the pattern, load the no. 4 round in Mink Tan and tip in Soft Peach. Pull in the comma stroke that forms this shape.

118

step 36] Load the no. 2 liner in Soft Peach. On the C-shaped scrolls, pull a long line that begins on the inside curve of one stroke marked "5" on the pattern. Continue it along the back of the C shape and up to the inside curve of the other stroke marked "5."

On the S-shaped scrolls, start the line on the inside curve of the stroke marked "5." Continue it along to out-line that side of the comma and contin-ue it on a little farther along the S.

Load the no. 00 liner in Soft Peach. Line the heads of the strokes marked "1" on the pattern with an M-shaped line. Pull in the curl and small comma strokes found at the base of the S-shaped scrolls.

Use a brush handle to dot French Mocha at the base of the S-shaped scroll.

step 37] For strokes marked "6" on the pattern, load the no. 2 round in Cash-mere Beige and tip in Soft Peach. Pull the comma strokes that form this fan shape back toward the dot.

Use a brush handle to dot mv. Brown where the comma strokes marked "6" converge.

Finishing

step 38] When the painting is com-plete, apply gold leafing on the outer surfaces of the tray and the feet, as instructed on page 66.

Pull the Krylon 18K Gold Leafing Pen along the top edge of the tray.

Erase any visible transfer lines.

Apply several coats of DecoArt Dura-Clear Satin Varnish to the entire surface with the 1-inch (25mm) basecoat/varnish brush.

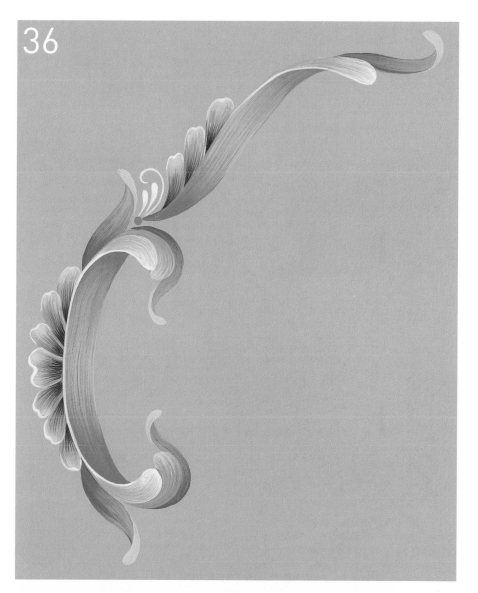

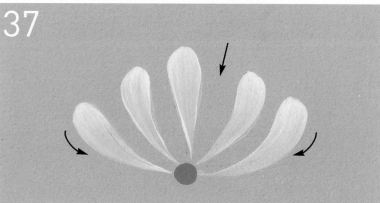

Completed Floral Tray

Gallery of Ideas

For detailed instructions on painting the projects in this gallery, contact Maureen McNaughton Enterprises. (See Resources on page 126.)

Counter Cubby

from Walnut Hollow, item 23568 (See Resources on page 126.)

DecoArt Americana Acrylic Paints

* indicates colors that DO NOT require extender

Khaki Tan (background color)

Pineapple, Moon Yellow

Reindeer Moss Green, Light Avocado, Evergreen, *Midnite Green, Mint Julep Green, Arbor Green, Hauser Dark Green

Wisteria, mv. Blue: Country Blue + touch of Gingerbread (to make it slightly duller), French Grey Blue, *Payne's Grey

*Deep Burgundy, *Black Plum

*Tangerine, *Pumpkin, Gingerbread, Burnt Orange

DecoArt Americana
Acrylic Paints

* indicates colors that DO NOT require extender

Warm Neutral + Mink Tan (1:1) (canister background color), Antique Teal + Black Green (4:1) (canister lid color)

Light Buttermilk, Buttermilk, Sand, *Lemon Yellow, Yellow Ochre

Reindeer Moss Green, Light Avocado, Arbor Green, *Midnite Green

lv. Blue Green: Antique Teal + Green Mist (5:1) , mv. Blue Green: Antique Teal + Green Mist (10:1), Black Green

lv. Blue: Blue Chiffon + Winter Blue (1:1), mv. Blue: French Grey Blue + Baby Blue (1:1), Uniform Blue, *Payne's Grey

French Mocha, Rookwood Red

Peach Sherbet, DeLane's Deep Shadow, *Brandy Wine

Khaki Tan, *Milk Chocolate, Burnt Sienna, Traditional Raw Umber, Lamp Black

Canister Set and Shelf

from Painters Paradise (See Resources on page 126.)

DecoArt Americana
Acrylic Paints

* indicates colors that DO NOT require extender

DM = DecoArt Dazzling Metallics
RM = DecoArt Royal Metallics

Soft Black (background color)

Moon Yellow, Golden Straw, Antique Gold, *Milk Chocolate

Olive Green, Light Avocado, Avocado, Evergreen, *Midnite Green

Sea Aqua, Arbor Green, *Deep Teal, Hauser Dark Green, lv. Blue: White Wash + Sapphire (3:1), Country Blue, Williamsburg Blue, *Payne's Grey

*Cranberry Wine, *Deep Burgundy, *Black Plum

*Tangerine, *Pumpkin, *Tangelo Orange, Burnt Orange, Georgia Clay

Gold Mix: Glorious Gold (DM) + Pale Gold (RM) (1:1)

Bisque Platter

from Duncan Enterprises (See Resources on page 126.)

Towel Holder with Rhododendrons

from Walnut Hollow, item 17231 (See Resources on page 126.)

DecoArt Americana Acrylic Paints

* indicates colors that DO NOT require extender

Desert Sand (background color), mv. Brown: Khaki Tan + Desert Sand (1:1) (faux finish color), *dv. Red: Deep Burgundy + Black Plum (4:1) (border color)

Sand, Pineapple, *Lemon Yellow, Moon Yellow, Golden Straw, True Ochre

Limeade, Celery Green, Light Avocado, Arbor Green, Evergreen, *Midnite Green,

*Coral Rose, *Antique Rose, *Country Red, *Deep Burgundy

*Peaches 'n' Cream, *Pumpkin, mv. Orange: Burnt Orange + True Ochre (1:1), Georgia Clay, Terra Cotta, *Russet, *Soft Black

DecoArt Americana Acrylic Paints

* indicates colors that DO NOT require extender

Driftwood, mv. Brown: Driftwood + Mississippi Mud (1:1), Mississippi Mud

Light Buttermilk, Buttermilk, French Vanilla, Moon Yellow, Camel, mv. Yellow: Honey Brown + Camel (1:1), *Honey Brown

Reindeer Moss Green, Celery Green, Light Avocado, mv. Green: Light Avocado + Neutral Grey (1:1), *Plantation Pine, *Midnite Green

Mint Julep Green, mv. Cool Green: Green Mist + touch of Antique Rose (to dull), Arbor Green, *Antique Teal, Hauser Dark Green

lv. Violet: Summer Lilac + Light Buttermilk (2:1), Summer Lilac, dv. Violet: Plum + touch of Charcoal Grey (to dull)

mv. Dull Violet: dv. Dull Violet + Khaki Tan (3:2), dv. Dull Violet: Plum + Charcoal Grey (3:1)

lv. Red: French Vanilla + French Mauve (1:1), French Mauve, Mauve, *Cranberry Wine, *Black Plum

Tin Box with Roses

from Painter's Paradise (See Resources on page 126.)

Resources

Surfaces

Duncan Enterprises
5673 East Shields Avenue
Fresno, CA 93727
Tel: 800-438-6226
www.duncanceramics.com

La Maison BeL'art
27 Mont-Plaisant
Morin-Heights, Quebec
Canada J0R 1H0
Tel: 450-226-5735
Fax: 450-226-5735
www.nvo.com/belarts

Painters Paradise
Jo C & Co.
111 Parrish Lane
Wilmington, DE 19810-3457
Tel: 302-478-7619
Fax: 302-478-9441
www.paintersparadise.com

Walnut Hollow
1409 State Road 23
Dodgeville, WI 53533
Tel: 1-800-395-5995
Fax: 608-935-3029
www.walnuthollow.com

Paints and Brushes

DecoArt Inc.
Stanford, KY 40484
Tel: 606-365-3193
Fax: 606-365-9739
E-mail: paint@decoart.com
www.decoart.com

**Maureen McNaughton
Enterprises Inc.**
(See listing under Canadian
Retailers.)

Organizations

**The Society
of Decorative Painters**
393 N. McLean Blvd.
Wichita, Kansas 67203-5968
www.decorativepainters.org

**The Canadian
Decorative Artists Network**
4981 Hwy. #7 East, Unit 12A
Suite 253
Markham, ON Canada
L3R 1N1
www.cdan.com

**The British Association of
Decorative & Folk Arts**
Margaret Nelson, BADFA
Membership Secretary,
6 Falcon Road
Horndean Waterloo
Hants England PO8 9BY

Canadian Retailers

Crafts Canada
2745 29th St. N.E.
Calgary, AL, T1Y 7B5

Folk Art Enterprises
P.O. Box 1088
Ridgetown, ON, N0P 2C0
Tel: 888-214-0062

**MacPherson
Craft Wholesale**
83 Queen St. E.
P.O. Box 1870
St. Mary's, ON, N4X 1C2
Tel: 519-284-1741

**Maureen McNaughton
Enterprises Inc.**
RR #2
Belwood, ON, N0B 1J0
Tel: 519-843-5648
Fax: 519-843-6022
E-mail:
maureen.mcnaughton.ent.
inc@sympatico.ca
www.maureenmc-
naughton.com

**Mercury Art
& Craft Supershop**
332 Wellington St.
London, ON, N6C 4P7
Tel: 519-434-1636

**Town & Country
Folk Art Supplies**
93 Green Lane
Thornhill, ON, L3T 6K6
Tel: 905-882-0199

U.K. Retailers

Art Express
Index House
70 Burley Road
Leeds LS3 1JX
0800 731 4185
www.artexpress.co.uk

Atlantis Art Materials
146 Brick Lane
London E1 6RU
020 7377 8855

Crafts World (head office)
No. 8 North Street
Guildford
Surrey GU1 4AF
07000 757070

Green & Stone
259 King's Road
London SW3 5EL
020 7352 0837
E-mail: greenandstone
@enterprise.net

Hobby Crafts (head office)
River Court
Southern Sector
Bournemouth International
Airport
Christchurch
Dorset BH23 6SE
0800 272387

Homecrafts Direct
PO Box 38
Leicester LE1 9BU
0116 251 3139

Index

More great painting instruction from North Light Books!

The Complete Book of Decorative Painting

This book is the must-have one-stop reference for decorative painters, crafters, home decorators and do-it-yourselfers. It's packed with solutions to every painting challenge, including surface preparation, lettering, borders, faux finishes, strokework techniques and more! You'll also find five fun-to-paint projects designed to instruct, challenge and entertain you—no matter what your skill level.

ISBN 1-58180-062-2, paperback
256 pages, #31803-K

Decorative Mini-Murals You Can Paint

Add drama to any room in your home with one of these eleven delightful mini-murals! They're perfect for when you don't have the time or the experience to tackle a whole wall. You'll learn exactly which colors and brushes to use, plus tips and mini-demos on how to get that realistic "wow" effect mural painters love. Detailed templates, photos and instructions assure your success at every step.

ISBN 1-58180-145-9, paperback
144 pages, #31891-K

How to Design Your Own Painting Projects

Let Michelle Temares show you how to develop, draw, transfer and paint your own original designs in seven easy-to-follow steps. "Good" and "bad" examples illustrate each important lesson, while three step-by-step decorative painting projects help you make the leap from initial idea to completed composition!

ISBN 1-58180-263-3, paperback
128 pages, #32128-K

Decorative Artist's Guide to Realistic Painting

Take your decorative painting to an exciting new level of depth and dimension by creating the illusion of reality that transforms your work from good to extraordinary! Patti DeRenzo, CDA, shows you how to master the building blocks of realism—value, temperature, intensity and form—to render three-dimensional images with height, depth and width.

ISBN 0-89134-995-2, paperback
128 pages, #31661-K

These books and other fine North Light titles are available from your local art & craft retailer, bookstore, online supplier or by calling 1-800-448-0915.